The Missed

Tales of Spirit

Tragic End at Niagara Falls

Written by Michelle Ann Kratts

Photographs by Michelle Petrazzoulo

To my most missed

Robert Frederick Barthel

Copyright 2013 © Michelle Ann Kratts

All rights reserved.

ISBN: 1493674811

ISBN-13: 978-1493674817

Table of Contents

Acknowledgements

Preface

Introduction

The Spirit of Niagara

Chapter One: In the Beginning

Chapter Two: Fascinated

Chapter Three: Paving the Way

Chapter Four: The Organization of Spiritualist Churches in Niagara Falls

Chapter Five: The Story of Dr. Henry Hardwicke

Ghosts

Chapter One: Lovely Place in Winter

Chapter Two: A Little Ghost Story to Commemorate the Life and Death (and the reawakening) of Captain Matthew Webb

Chapter Three: Another Homeless Ghost

Death Sketches

Chapter One: A Dreadful End; Elmira Millard

Chapter Two: Forgotten Sleeps; Emily Helena Crummer Lodge

Chapter Three: Niagara's Lost Lovers; Lottie Philpott and Ethelbert Parsons

Chapter Four: The Silver Drinking-cup of Death; Mathilde Rolland

Chapter Five: The Cementation of the Dead; Theodore Graves Hulett

Chapter Six: Little Miss Rough-on-Rats; Minnie Scott

Chapter Seven: Will the real Maud Willard please stand up? Maud Willard

Chapter Eight: She was Demented; Caroline Rank

Last Lines

Bibliography

The author and the photographer

Acknowledgements

Our sincerest gratitude to so many people who have provided information and especially to those who have shared their stories. To Peter Ames (my partner in crime) for all of his research assistance and for finding so many of the missed; Jimmy and Lisa Silvaroli, Amy Wall and the rest of NF Paranormal for your interesting perspective on the paranormal; Joe Morock for your valuable technical expertise; Amy Koban (thank you for your insight during an interview many years ago); Tom Tryniski, the god of New York history, at www.fultonhistory.com for providing free access to a treasure trove of New York history; Cynthia Melcher for assistance with the story of Vine Hickox; the Crummer and Lodge families for assistance with the story of Emily Lodge; Lori Y. for assistance with the story of Minnie Scott; the Niagara Falls City Clerk's office for numerous death records; Tim Baxter for providing a special outlet for my stories on www.myoakwoodcemetery.com ; Chris Stoianoff for providing a special outlet for my stories on www.niagarahub.com ; the local libraries…especially the Lewiston Public Library and the Niagara Falls Public Library for keeping history alive and available; the staff, board and volunteers at Oakwood Cemetery, Niagara Falls, New York--Niagara's official caretaker of the world's most unusual garden of stories; to our families and friends for providing tea and cupcakes and doughnuts…and finally to the missed of Niagara Falls.

A special thanks to Michelle Petrazzoulo, my friend and the director of the Niagara Falls Public Library, for amusing walks in the cemetery and for bringing these stories to life through her beautiful photography.

Preface

Many of these stories began as scribbles on a napkin. I just didn't want to forget them. I find it sad that people are forgotten through death and time. All that remains are the urns that hold our ashes, a tombstone...and a story. I tried to gather a bouquet of history, legends, ghosts and tragedies from Niagara. The section, The Spirit of Niagara, explains Niagara's unique history of spirit. The section, Ghosts, contains stories I contrived with my own imagination—although they contain true local historical characters. The Matthew Webb story came about after I read an actual account in an old Niagara Falls Gazette of the encounter. The section, Death Sketches, involves stories of tragic end in Niagara. Some stories are short and bittersweet, other stories were much more personal to me—such as the story of Emily Lodge. The final section of this book, Last Lines, contains lines from a few of the letters that have been found at Niagara Falls following suicides.

Many of these stories had other incarnations through my column at www.myoakwoodcemetery.com and on www.niagarahub.com.

I think there really is magic in Niagara Falls. I think this really is the edge of the world. And these stories are, in essence, contrived by Niagara, herself, for none would be possible without her.

Introduction

I felt as if I could have gone over with the waters; it would be so beautiful a death.

Harriet Beecher Stowe

If you are close enough you know she is there in the morning. From my little bed in an old brick house on Pierce Avenue I could hear her voice first; a trillion whispers caught in a web. Even before I felt the rhythm of my breath, the ticking of the clock, the clutter of the birds in the lilac tree... there was Niagara. She was somehow connected to the light and the flow of energy that brought the day to life. She had arms that surrounded me and strong legs and she would run into my dreams and twist them into nightmares.

I will always mistrust water because of her. I used to imagine I was a part of the drama that unfolded at the brink. So close to the edge the water is smooth and clear. She teases you. She covers you in her perfume and you see yourself giving in at the end. So many have given in and their voice is a perfect chorus. Once, I saw a Hasidic Jew climb over the rails. He dropped to his knees and prayed like I have never seen anyone pray. There was a tempest whirling in his tendrils and the rest of us held our breath. He did not waver. His folded hands were still. Eventually the Parks Police coaxed him back to the other side. He didn't jump. Just *another crazy*! We all breathed a sigh of relief for it's such a messy thing when it happens. But in some strange corner of our minds we envied him for having been in that other place—on the other side of the rails.

We, who live here, whose families have been here for generations, have our own stories. Many years ago, another Mrs. Kratts made the headlines when she took a cab from her neat little home on 81st Street, left her shoes and her purse on the riverbank and jumped in. This other Mrs. Kratts (Mylrae, my husband's aunt) had been stalking Niagara for quite some time. It seemed the perfect setting for her demise. And so she let herself go into Niagara's swirling arms and as if merely a reveler at a carnival, she went for a wild ride. No struggle. Only movement, broken sparks of light, watery peace. Fortunately, her ride was cut short when a fireman caught sight of that horror of horrors—a woman in the river—and jumped in to save her. She fought him, scratched at him, beat her fists against his chest. She tried to get her thin wrists out from under his grasp. But he was well-trained in these waters. He politely ignored her pleas for freedom. And, of course, he adhered to the fact that it is never proper to let a lady go over the falls—at any cost—even if it meant he would have to go over to try to save her.

Ultimately he saved her and received many awards for his heroism…and the other Mrs. Kratts did not go over the falls after all.

Some who come to Niagara are weaker and they leave us in this way. Still for others departure seems to be accidental. There is a sort of temporary madness that is scattered in her mist. I will never be able to forget the woman who *lost her balance* and dropped her infant into the white death. She said she was under a spell; completely irresponsible for her actions. Those who work on the boat docks of the Maid of the Mist know about the weaker ones and the magic spells for they surface in that area or near Youngstown at Fort Niagara. Bodies bloated, stripped and tangled in seaweed and sand wash upon the shore quite regularly. They are souvenirs from ill-fated trips to Niagara Falls. And then there are the others who disappear completely--no pieces left behind and it is as if they never existed at all.

Niagara, by nature, though beautiful and serene, can be horrible and deadly. She is a paradox and the city that grew around her is not anything at all like the cities, villages and towns that sleep quietly beside her. She is misunderstood, abused, the brunt of jokes, *"one of the greatest curiosities of the world."* She is a *"goddess"*—an inspiration for divine love. Ancient legend reveals her base to be the home of the Great Spirit. She is a healer and with her magic many human ills have been cured. A work of art, travelers have come for centuries to view her in her strange museum. And, we too, are travelers. We bring our friends to see her. We stop for a time, enjoy the scenery, leave a bit of us behind—a shoe, a ring, a dusty pair of sunglasses—then return to where we came from. Niagara is the story of travelers and tourists. None of us really belong here at all. This is her kingdom of tragedy and mist—a kingdom set at the edge of the world. And these are her stories.

The Spirit of Niagara

Some years ago the great Niagara caused those living within sound of the roar of its waters to awake, not because of its noise, but because of its silence...

Carrie E. S. Twing, 1898

Chapter One

In the Beginning

Some believe there is no death, only rebirth, and there are places where there is a communion between these two worlds. Niagara is said to be one of these locations for there is a phenomenon here that is peculiar to all places of intense beauty. Peter A. Porter said it was the presence of Deity, or Spirit. Others find Niagara a *"power point"* of energy. Amy Koban, a practicing medium from Niagara Falls, describes falling water as a natural root cause for paranormal activity. Regardless of our combinations of language, it seems undeniable that the veil between the living and the dead is very thin here. This strange duality of forces—at once divinely beautiful, yet at the same time terrifyingly violent and the embodiment of our greatest fears—has intrigued people for centuries. There is a hypnotic effect that Niagara stamps upon the soul. Some have to tear away from the brink as they feel themselves becoming helpless to their urges. It was inevitable that Niagara would become a haven for the poet, the artist and the mystic. They were the *"Sky Holders,"* the Medicine Men, translators of the Divine.

Ever since the very beginning when Father Louis Hennepin, a Recollect missionary who had accompanied LaSalle on the expedition of 1678, wrote the first lengthy account of the falls—*"that dreadful gulf (where) one is seized with horror,"* people have understood there would be hazards associated with a trip to Niagara. However, it was not only the cataract itself that presented horrific dangers. Early travelers' accounts describe a rugged and ancient wilderness where Nature and her beasts ruled supreme. There were wolves that roamed in packs of 20 or 30 at a time and *"were so fierce as to attack men in the middle of the day."* In the summer months it was said that one may *"meet with rattlesnakes at every step and Musquitoes swarm so thickly in the air…that you might cut them with a knife…* A Herefordshire man and guide told one traveler that the rattlesnakes were of such an enormous girth that he had once killed one containing twenty-four rattles. It was truly a nightmarish landscape.

And yet there were also rainbows that spread across the daytime skies in Biblical proportions and moon visions that glimmered through the mist. At one time rainbows were present each morning from ten until noon. John Quincy Adams remarked that *"it takes away all language as well as thought, and in this raptured condition one is almost capable of prophesying—standing as it were in a trance, unable to speak."*

The moon was a bedtime story in itself as it hovered-- wonderful and curious-- above the Niagara River. One hot summer evening in 1787 an English captain who had been visiting Fort Schlosser and the Stedman's stopped before the gates of the Fort upon noticing the moon. Never in his travels had he seen such a sight as the magic around the setting moon over Niagara. It appeared *"to rise to a very uncommon height in likeness to a very dark column."* He had witnessed a moon bow, or a lunar bow, a rare phenomenon produced when light reflects off the surface of the moon and shines upon the mist created by the waterfalls. They are unlikely to occur today because there is less water and therefore less mist due to the diversion of water for electrical purposes and because of the many city lights that crowd up the night sky. At one time, the Maid of the Mist would make moonlight trips for the sole purpose of allowing travelers the opportunity to view the lunar bows. It is not hard to understand how Niagara's unusual and remarkable landscape captivated the early travelers.

One special visitor, who will forever be connected with Niagara's mystical past, was Francis Abbott, the Hermit of Niagara. Tall and handsome, wearing a loose gown or cloak of chocolate brown, he was first seen passing through Niagara Falls on the afternoon of June 18, 1829. His singular appearance caught the eye of all who had looked upon him. Carrying only a roll of blankets, a flute, a portfolio, a large book and a small stick, he walked into the hotel and asked the landlady the usual questions about the falls and then about where he might find a library. Immediately, he found his way to the library where he proceeded to borrow some music books and purchase a violin. The librarian was informed that his name was Francis

Abbott...and the rest is local folklore and history. Increasingly, he became completely and utterly bewitched by the falls. He found his way to the library often and each time he spoke with the librarian he informed him that he would be staying a little longer than he had originally planned.

The proprietor of the island allowed him to stay at the only dwelling then on the island where a family lived. He ate very little and lived the life of a monk. He lived such as this for about twenty months and would often be seen with his guitar, supported with a silken sash, walking the banks of the whirlpool. His music was strange to the ears of those who listened. They came from their homes and he would just as soon walk away.

Eventually, as time went on, he built a cottage of his own near the high bank of the river—in full view of the falls. He lived here about two months with only a cat and his pet dog. Much of his time was spent in quiet solitude and meditation. Many grew accustomed to his peculiarities—how he loved to bathe in the cascades between Goat Island and the Three Sisters Islands, even in the coldest weather, and how he made a daily practice of walking over a piece of timber that extended over the Terrapin Rocks and 12-15 feet over the precipice of the falls—sometimes hanging over the chasm by his hands and feet for fifteen minute intervals. He was known to write quite often, mostly in Latin, but destroyed his works just as fast as he created them.

Francis Abbott disappeared on June 10, 1831. The last person to see him was the ferryman at 2:00 in the afternoon. Only his clothes were found on the rocks. On June 21, his body was identified at Fort Niagara. The next day he was interred in the burial ground at Niagara Falls. He was eventually removed to Oakwood Cemetery and his gravesite remains one of the most popular sites. Following his death, an inscription was found chiseled upon a rock on Luna Island and believed to have been written by Abbott, himself: *All is Change, Eternal Progress, No Death*. He was about 28 years of age at the time of his death and a most spectacular curiosity and precursor to the spiritual history of Niagara Falls.

Another most singular individual who found his way to Niagara was Godfrey N. Frankenstein. Born in Hesse-Darmstadt, Germany, in 1820, he would become *"the painter of Niagara Falls."* It was said that as a child he was so strange as to gleefully await the slaughter of the pigs on his father's farm so that he might *"collect a quantity of blood for paint."* And just as Francis Abbott had been enamored of Niagara, young Frankenstein found himself *"so charmed with their grandeur and beauty"* that he spent much of his life in Niagara Falls and painting the scenery. He developed a growing fascination, or *"almost an obsession with Niagara Falls."* He *"made the study of the great cataract a labor of love."* He summered and wintered by it. Painted it by day and by night; capturing every angle and each nuance. He was well known even to paint as *"the grey rocks wore an icy robe and the spray congealed into icicles upon his stiffened garments."*

Although he painted over one hundred easel paintings of the falls, he is most well-known for his panorama, *"Niagara."* *"Niagara"* was painted upon a strip of canvas that was over 1,000 feet long and nine feet high. It rolled from one wooden spindle to the next, with the assistance of Frankenstein's siblings who had helped to arrange the panels systematically. It was first exhibited in the old City Hall in Springfield, Ohio, before touring much of the country. Some historians believe that Frankenstein's panorama of Niagara was the very first inception of a motion picture. The panorama was unique as it provided a sort of *"cinematic"* effect as its size and portrayals made viewers feel as if they were swallowed up into the giant cataract, themselves. There was music and drama to accompany its viewing. It grew to intense popularity. *"Owing to the increased desire to see this remarkable work of art and to enable ladies and children to see it, Frankenstein's Moving Panorama of Niagara will hereafter be exhibited both morning and night...admission 50 cents."*

Frankenstein had also included inserts of terror, such as the collapse of the Table Rock and a boatman's fatal plunge—which horrified, as well as entertained, the viewers. Commentators were well aware of the strong theme of death which prevailed throughout much of Frankenstein's work on Niagara. *"The spectre of death seemed implicated in the medium's own mode of representation; like a cadaver...the canvas resembles a living being...and yet there is a paradox in the close resemblance to death..."*

Truly, a panorama such as *"Niagara"* was a giant among works of art and Niagara was the perfect subject. The artist at Niagara had become not unlike the *"Sky Holder,"* or interpreter of the divine.

Frankenstein died from a cold on February 24, 1873. He is buried in Spring Grove Cemetery in Cincinnati. Unfortunately the behemoth panorama, *"Niagara,"* is also gone. It is believed that he had stored it in Black's Opera House in Springfield which burned to the ground in 1903. *"Whatever its merit, it no doubt long ago passed into the limbo of the forgotten."*

Chapter Two

Fascinated

The mid-19th century swept through western New York with a frenzy that had never been seen before. There were new emotions arising as the dust settled from the late wars and as a new nation sought to create a persona. The Frankenstein panorama was noted as being a true representation of our nationhood. It portrayed an indomitable and reckless spirit—the passion and pathos of the American-- in its panels of Niagara Falls. There was an incessant longing in the American for an understanding of this strange new position, an identity, among the nations of the world. Much of western New York was still frontier and spiritual needs were often left unanswered as clergy were scarce. Folk movements grew at an alarming pace. The grounds were fertile for an awakening. Niagara was a part of what became known as the "*Burned Over District.*" This term referred to the section of the country where new religions were founded and it was tied in closely with other movements such as the Women's Rights Movement and Abolitionism. It was not too far from Niagara, in Palmyra, New York, where Joseph Smith was said to have been visited by the angel, Moroni, and the Latter Day Saint religion was born. The Millerites, the Shakers and various Utopian experiments were coming to life and gaining a stronghold in this region. Most importantly, on March 31, 1848, the modern Spiritualist movement was born when the Fox sisters in Hydesville, New York, began communicating with "*Mr. Splitfoot,*" the spirit of a peddler who had been murdered and buried under their home. Perhaps it was merely a coincidence that the day before the event in Hydesville, on March 30, 1848, the great Falls at Niagara were silenced because of a natural phenomenon that sent many panicking that the end of the world was coming. An ice jam had temporarily cut the flow of the water. Eventually a crack formed and the water was flowing again, but not before hundreds of fascinated people ventured out in the riverbed.

And Niagara *did* fascinate. Here, the space between heaven and earth was quite visibly smaller. Niagara was a symbol for the fugitive slave of the great power of the promise of freedom. Thousands made their way to this border-land with Canada and found new life just a stone's throw across the water. However, it was also a point of energetic conflict as Niagara was the location at which bounty hunters sought their rewards. There were local men and women within the community who assisted in the Underground Railroad, and there were those who profited from assisting the bounty hunters.

It was no secret that the Abolitionist movement was deeply embedded in Spiritualism. Prominent leaders such as Harriet Beecher Stowe, William Lloyd Garrison and Thomas Garrett were professed Spiritualists. Many fugitives were brought to freedom through Niagara by Harriet Tubman, an intensely spiritual woman, herself. She was known to have been led by dream visions, to have spoken to God, Himself. Many knew her to be a *"firm believer in spiritual manifestations."* In fact, her biographer, Sarah Bradford, had a difficult time portraying her character as she tried desperately to limit revealing her strange behaviors and beliefs for she was certain that its mere mention could possibly discredit her.

By the 1850's and 1860's, well known psychics, such as Emma Hardinge Britten, were coming to Niagara. *"By spirit direction we visited Niagara Falls and Rochester, at both these places our spirit friends made important declarations."*

In 1850, the *Spiritual Philosopher* pondered the idea of the *"fascination with a sense of danger...Persons may be fascinated with beauty, music, gold or the love of money; and also by the sense of dangers."* It went on to tell of a young lady, who had been so *"fascinated"* looking over the precipice at Niagara Falls that she lost her self-control and was *"dashed to pieces on the rocks below."* Persons in this state should be *"Pathetized, and thus the spell may be broken..."* And over the years this *"fascination"* continued to ignite many desperate souls. We find the same story in our papers, over and over again. Different names, different walks of life, but the same sentiment of death.

An event in December of 1855 brought the Spiritualism debate to the forefront in Niagara Falls. A popular lecture series held at the Odd Fellows Hall included a Spiritualist speaker *"and the subject was handled without gloves."* The debate grew to such proportions that another series of lectures was held just about a month later *"against Modern Spiritualism"* at the Clarendon Hotel. Professor Grimes, the *"father of the humbug,"* discussed *"the rise and progress of Spiritualism,"* and went on to other topics such as *"how mediums are made"* and *"how the so-called spiritual manifestations were produced."* Interestingly, the editors at the Niagara Falls Gazette did not seem to completely approve of Dr. Grimes' rebuttal of the Spiritualists.

"Professor Grimes has only partially explained the humbug...it only proves that the day may not be far...when science will dispel any other clouds which may now apparently surround the subject."

Ironically, it would not be too far into the future when science, itself, would begin to tap into a whole new set of inquiries and when the *scientists,* themselves, would become the leaders of the Spiritualist movement.

Perhaps the Civil War had one of the greatest effects upon the Spiritualist history of Niagara Falls. It was the largest mass loss of life that the United States had ever experienced and Niagara was not immune. Many of her sons were lost on the battlefield. Spiritualism filled the void for some as it proclaimed that death was not the end; there is survival for man. Even Mary Todd Lincoln, the president's wife, and a frequent visitor who spent some time at the Cataract House in Niagara Falls, was known to have held séances at the White House.

It had finally become mainstream and fashionable to contact the dead. The Victorian era also brought forth a *romantification* of death. A front page obituary from the Daily Gazette reveals more of a ghost story than a death notice as it describes a striking graveside incident. It was written that, as the minister began to read the passage "... *"I heard a voice from Heaven, a roll of thunder from the gathering clouds hushed his voice and added an impressive solemnity to the occasion, which was the more notable as it was the only time the clouds gave forth their voice."* It was during this time that Lily Dale Assembly, the world's largest and most popular Spiritualist community was founded in the Town of Pomfret, just a short distance from Niagara Falls.

Another shocking story appeared several years later when the Niagara Gazette reported in bold headlines... *"MAID OF THE MIST CREW SAW GHOSTS."*

Sailors from the famous steamboat company had become *"greatly concerned"* as each evening they were witness to a most unusual scene involving *"weird lights"* around the eddies of the river near the Canadian wharfs. The sailors began to believe it *"must be the ghosts of the drowned haunting the scene of their dissolution."* After Captain R.F. Carter, commander of the boat, saw the weird lights and was puzzled, himself, he decided to investigate.

He came up with an extremely complex explanation involving a wooden tub filled with phosphorescent paint in which drift wood would come into contact with and coincidentally catch fire if the driftwood would happen to toss upon another object, float around, dry in the sun, and break open.

It is likely that the sailors stuck with their original theory of ghosts—as it, quite frankly, made more sense.

**It may be interesting to note that a news article printed alongside the above "MAID OF THE MIST CREW SAW GHOSTS" contained a report stating that the very same day, July 11th, the crew of the Maid of the Mist secured "a most ghastly object" from the shore of Lake Ontario...a human leg that had been torn from the body at the hip, still wearing a stocking and shoe.

Chapter Three

Paving the Way

With the advent of modern science, so came the need for the *scientific explanation* of a paranormal event. The scientists who first discovered the unseen worlds of radio waves and other new technologies began to find themselves wondering about other unseen worlds, as well, for their discoveries revealed that they had proven there are, indeed, invisible layers of existence. Thus the *Society for Psychical Research* (SPR) was founded in England in 1882.

It was the first society formed for the purpose of investigating *"that large body of debatable phenomena designated by such terms as mesmeric, psychical and "spiritualistic", and to do so "in the same spirit of exact and unimpassioned enquiry which has enabled Science to solve so many problems."* Its founders and members included an illustrious list of Cambridge and Oxford philosophers, physicists, chemists, psychologists, criminologists and physicians. There were Nobel Prize winners, the founder of the League of Nations, and even a man who would one day become the prime minister of England. Some of the more popular members included C.J. Jung, Sir Arthur Conan Doyle and Sir Oliver Lodge, a pioneer of wireless technology and radio, who would ultimately forge a unique tie, himself, to Niagara Falls. Spiritualism seemed to have struck a chord within the heart of its strongest enemy—the scientist-- and things would never be the same. It wouldn't be long before one of the world's most brilliant scientists made his mark upon Niagara and changed the way we live. His name was Nikola Tesla and everyone who has been to Niagara Falls knows how great a man he was for his figure alone has been memorialized into a bronze statue at the State Park.

Tesla was most unusual for in some strange way the spirit of Niagara seemed to reach across the world and into a little Croatian town, where as a precocious young boy, he had a dream that would change the course of history. *"I was fascinated by a description of Niagara Falls...and pictured in my imagination a big wheel run by the falls..."* His obsessions with Niagara would one day electrify the world. In 1895, the first great hydroelectric power plant in the world was built with patents for generators for polyphase currents from Nikola Tesla, in Niagara Falls, New York. The great power, the spirit of Niagara Falls, was harnessed to create electricity that could light up places near and far and the basic idea had been conceived from a boyhood dream.

There are many other stories about Tesla's peculiar character and his belief that Niagara was indeed a power point of energy and communication with other realms of life forces. In the early 1900's Mr. Tesla was reportedly *"preparing to hail Mars with Niagara's voice."* Niagara's power companies would cooperate by projecting an 800 million horse power message over the 100 million mile gulf between the earth and Mars. It is believed that as he, indeed, received responses to these communications, they were the sound waves emitted from a distant planet though not actually an intelligent communication.

While Niagara was paving the world with light and energy, simultaneously the most massive movement of people to the Niagara area was taking place. Thousands of immigrants from southern and eastern Europe and from lands as far off as Lebanon, Turkey and Armenia flooded every entrance into Niagara Falls. The author William Feder wrote in his landmark work that *"Niagara Falls became known for having the highest percentage of immigrants of any city in New York State outside of New York City."* Many of these immigrants brought alongside their suitcases a bit of the darkness, the shadows, from an old and ancient world. They brought their own intense spiritual folklore and superstitions; stories that became forever enmeshed into the history of Niagara. The southern Italians in Niagara Falls brought their ghosts, their fortune tellers and their great fear of "mal occhio" or the Evil Eye. They consulted one another about dream visions, premonitions and demonic possessions. Roman Catholic priests conducted *"exorcisms."*

The Armenians, who had faced intolerable death and misery before coming to America, had similar traditions. They often wore blue beads to protect against the *"Evil Eye,"* and had various spell and curse breaking phrases such as *"God be with you,"* or *"Mashalah."* The

Armenians were also proficient at reading the tea leaves at the bottom of their Turkish coffee. For them, the loss had been so recent and so great that perhaps the space between living and dead was ever smaller. Many of the other immigrant groups who made Niagara their home had similar superstitions and it was not too far of a stretch for them to comprehend the basic ideas of Spiritualism, for their own indigenous cultures had cultivated similar beliefs for hundreds of years.

Chapter Four
The Organization of Spiritualist Churches in Niagara Falls

By the dawn of the 20th century Spiritualist churches were steadily organizing throughout the United States and especially within the city of Niagara Falls. The National Spiritualist Association, founded in 1893 by Cora L.V. Scott, a medium and trance lecturer (as well as an abolitionist in earlier years) who lived in Buffalo for a time, was established in Niagara Falls as the First Spiritualist Association.

In January of 1903 the Niagara Falls Gazette advertised that a Spiritualist medium and adviser from Buffalo, *"Mrs. Atcheson,"* would be *"at the home of Mrs. Onan, cor. Pine and 29th all day Wednesday, January 7th, for personal readings."* Proceeds would benefit the Spiritualist Association of Niagara Falls. It went on to read that a Séance Circle would also be held that same evening at the Maccabees Hall, 2207 Main Street. It is believed that this event may have represented the birth of the first officially organized Spiritualist Church in Niagara Falls. Previous to the inception of the First Spiritualist Church, most practiced privately within their homes and even following the creation of organized churches a great majority of Spiritualists preferred to practice in such a manner (particularly, the new immigrants who continued to read tea leaves and interpret dreams at their own kitchen tables).

Mrs. Ellen Onan, the hostess of the day-long event in 1903, had come to Niagara Falls *"to take advantage of the job opportunities created by the expanding electrical industry following her husband's death in 1900."* She was the mother of three young boys, as well as a nurse. Descendants may be curious as to the true reasons for the young widow's sudden move to Niagara Falls. Family records reveal, among other tidbits, that she had at one time *"taught school in Cuba, NY, which was not far from (her husband's hometown of) Allegany."* It is just conjecture, but it is possible that it may have been at this point that Ellen became infused with Spiritualism for the founder of the National Spiritualist Association, Cora L.V. Scott, one of the most prominent and influential women in the Spiritualist movement, a woman who had revealed her craft as medium at the White House for President Lincoln, was born in Cuba.

This section of New York was aflutter with Spiritualism during this time period.

Lily Dale Assembly, established in 1879, was only about 50 miles away from where a 20 year old Ellen would have been teaching. It is also possible that Ellen had become interested in Spiritualism as a comfort following the grief of the loss of loved ones. She, herself, may have been witness to great human tragedy as a child, as well, for she had been born in 1858 in Richmond, Virginia, just a few short years before the onset of the Civil War. For southerners, the Civil War had been a horror not too far from home.

Niagara Falls had clearly become an important location for the national Spiritualist community. In January, the New York State Spiritualist Association gathered at the Maccabees Hall for a *"most important"* meeting. Vine H. Hickox, a pioneer of Niagara Falls, wrote several lengthy pieces that were published in the newspaper about Spiritualism, the spirit messages and concerning Mrs. Atcheson's discourses. Ella Atcheson, the wife of a Buffalo baker, was Niagara's First Spiritualist Church's founding minister. People came from quite the distance to hear her speak and to benefit from her mediumship. Hickox often gave specific and emotional examples of her incredible work. He wrote of the large crowds of desperate Niagarans longing to reconnect with their deceased loved ones. He described the ideals of Spiritualism through Rev. Atcheson's own words…*"Spiritualism not only has opened the door between the mortal and the immortal…it has spread the truth…it is freeing the minds of men and women from doubt and error…"*

Mr. Hickox, himself a follower of a form of Christian Spiritualism, wrote of the *"whispers of dear departed friends…of mortals touched by their loved ones who are ministering angels…"* He explained the basic tenets of Spiritualism to the general public as follows:

Spiritualism asserts that the soul spirit is the real man; the natural body is but the medium through which the soul of man interprets itself to its fellows.…

His family believes that the loss of his own dear wife while still quite young may have been the catalyst for his fervent embracing of Spiritualism. He also wrote in an article, dated February 6, 1907, *"The Benefit of Spiritualism,"* that his own father had been a *"strong adherent to the Methodist Church, fond of reading the old family bible and having prayers in his home…"* However, his mother, Mercia Harrington Hickox, *"did not have so much interest in those exercises, in fact she seemed to feel glad when the family prayers were over…."* He went on to say that she *"could read people seemingly in a Psychic way and prophesy."* Ironically, Mrs. Hickox had a great mistrust of Niagara, herself, as the river had taken one of her children to a watery grave.

On a sultry summer's evening in July of 1907, less than a year before Mr. Hickox became one of the departed, a large audience attended a gathering at the Maccabees Hall in order to receive a message *"from some loved one in the spirit land."* He went on to add that *"this phrase of mediumship is becoming very interesting to many in this city….they begin to realize the truth of the continuity of life, after the death of the mortal body."* On April 21, 1908, Vine H. Hickox entered the spirit land, himself.

Other Spiritualist churches grew out of the First Spiritualist Church of Niagara Falls. Some adhered to a more Christian sort of Spiritualism, whereas others focused on the more titillating aspects of mediumship. The Progressive Spiritual Church of Truth began meeting at Whirlpool Street, at No. 933 Main Street opposite the Armory and eventually at the Unitarian Church at 639 Main Street. The Spiritual Tabernacle met at the IOOF Hall on South Avenue, near Main Street. The Trinity Spiritualist Church met at the corner of Ashland and Main Street and at 320 6th Street. The Unity Spiritualist Church met at Silberberg's Hall, between Main Street and Niagara Avenue. The Center of Psychic Spiritualists met at the Hotel Niagara in Room A, and the White Rose Center of Free Psychic Truth which had been active throughout the 1940's held their services in the basement of the Unitarian Church. These churches opened their doors to people of all faiths and backgrounds. *All are welcome,* was commonly added to the advertisements. They offered lectures such as *"Angel Ministrations," "The Force of Spirit,"* and *"Psychic Teaching for Adults and Children."* Messages were given, as well as the reading of sealed ballots, clairvoyance, healing services, worship, psychic classes, unfoldment (meditation) classes and much more. Message, or séance, circles were usually held afterwards or at various mediums' homes. Often prominent psychics and mediums came to Niagara Falls for ballot reading sessions. T. John Kelly, a noted Spiritualist medium associated with Lily Dale, came to the Spiritualist Tabernacle at the IOOF Temple, on South Avenue, near Main Street, Niagara Falls in 1932. He was considered the *"premier in this phase of psychic phenomenon"* and his presence in Niagara Falls would *"open the door (to) the spirit world, where... loved ones are anxiously waiting to communicate..."*

Chapter Five

The Story of

Dr. Henry Hardwicke

Perhaps the most intriguing stories concerning Niagara's Spiritualist past involve an obscure physician and psychologist named Dr. Henry Hardwicke. Born in Niagara Falls to Major Alan H. G. Hardwicke (a native of England and the only thirty-third degree Mason in Niagara Falls at the time of his death and burial at Oakwood Cemetery) and Henrietta Ware (a descendant of a Revolutionary War veteran who also lies buried in Oakwood Cemetery), Dr. Hardwicke's serious inclinations toward the paranormal may have begun to fully awaken during his service as an Army Medical Officer in the First World War. World War I, with its catastrophic bloodshed, inspired yet another generation to seek communication with their newly deceased loved ones. It is possible that it was during his service in the war that Dr. Hardwicke came into contact with another physician, Dr. Le Roy Crandon, who was said to have had a *"morbid obsession with mortality"* and a certain charming and enigmatic civilian volunteer ambulance driver, from Ontario, Mina Stinson Crandon (Dr. Crandon's notorious wife) also known in Spiritualist circles as *Margery the Medium*. Another source describes the fact that Dr. Hardwicke and Dr. Crandon had a history of practicing together as physicians *"in the same neighborhood"* (in Niagara Falls?) or possibly there had been some connection through Mina, *"well known here…,"* (in Niagara Falls) and a cousin of a prominent Niagara Falls resident, the attorney, A. W. Gray. Regardless of how these three individuals were originally connected, they met here in Niagara Falls and they gained worldwide attention for their investigations into the spirit realms and for stumping Harry Houdini. Together, they would shake the very foundation of Spiritualism.

Dr. Harkwicke's destiny was to ultimately play a special part in the Spiritualist history of Niagara Falls. It would not be the first time his family made local history. The great great grandson of Jesse Ware, noted as the first American born white settler of Niagara Falls, Dr. Hardwicke's family was quite respected in these parts. Just a young man, Henry Hardwicke may have been present that day in September of 1903 when his mother provided the carriages to convey guests to Oakwood Cemetery where the Daughters of the American Revolution placed a tombstone to commemorate his grandfather's service in the Revolutionary War. Jesse Ware, a native of New Braintree, Massachusetts, had "*shouldered a gun with the Minute Men and went forth to battle at the sound of the alarm from Lexington*" and then some years later was summoned to Niagara by a friend (or relative), John Stedman, who had been the master of the very important portage. Following in his grandfather's footsteps, Dr. Hardwicke found himself a traveler on a new frontier--one that was just as mystical and unknown as Niagara.

As a boy, young Henry was already making the headlines in Niagara Falls. In 1894, he and his friend, Richard Carey, organized a "*well-managed affair*" on Jefferson Avenue. The bicycle race, which began on Jefferson Avenue in front of St. Peter's Church followed a course down Jefferson Avenue to Quay Street, down Quay to Erie Avenue, down Erie to First Street and then back to Jefferson Avenue. Boys from all corners of the city "*flocked to the spot*" and had a thoroughly enjoyable time of it. John O'Donnell was first place winner. Henry presented him with a "*handsome silver medal*". His father, A.G.H. Hardwicke, quite possibly had provided the prize which may have come from his hardware store, Hardwicke and Co., located on Falls Street.

As an adult Henry received a medical degree from Hahnemann Medical College in Philadelphia and served in the Army Medical Services during World War I. He practiced as a physician for a time in both Niagara Falls and Erie, Pennsylvania. He was a member of the Niagara Players and portrayed interesting and psychologically complex personalities for productions at the Capitol Theatre. In December of 1917, he was elected Worshipful Master of Niagara Frontier Lodge, No. 132, F. & A. M. Like his father, he had obtained high and mystical ranking as a devoted member of the local chapter of the Free Masons. During the 1920's he worked as the manager of the Equitable Life Assurance Society of the United States, located in an office building on Falls Street, and frequently gave talks on various insurance related matters.

By the 1930's, however, Dr. Hardwicke had become a full - fledged Spiritualist. He had written at least one book, *Voices From Beyond*, which was published in 1930 by the Harkell Co., in Niagara Falls, and had travelled extensively on the lecturing circuit.

His subjects included things such as *"The Lure of Adventure to the Fourth Dimensional Realms,"* use of the camera in psychic research, the direct voice, levitation and cross correspondence. He believed he was sensitive to a disembodied spirit named Walter—a very popular spirit at the time as he was known to show up at Mina Crandon's séances, too. Walter, the ghostly guide, was supposedly Walter Stinson, a young man who died at Onset Station after being crushed on board the railroad cars near Boston on August 6, 1911. He was also Mina Stinson Crandon's brother.

The spirit of Walter was the driving force behind several very famous experiments which took place concurrently between groups of Spiritualists in both Boston (at 10 Lyme Street—the home of Dr. Le Roy and Mina Crandon) and in Niagara Falls (the home of Dr. Henry and Katherine Hardwicke).

"An experiment in cross-correspondence between Dr. H.S.W. Hardwicke, ...Fifty-seventh Street, well known Niagara Falls medium, and Margery, the Boston medium, was reported by Dr. L.R.G. Crandon, husband of Margery, at the meeting of the New York section of the American Society for Psychical Research in Boston. Dr. Crandon reported that séances had been held simultaneously by Dr. Hardwicke in Niagara Falls and Margery in Boston and that an identical thumbprint was made in wax at both places almost simultaneously by Walter, the spirit control of Margery..."

Other events involving Walter took place at Dr. Hardwicke's home, as well. Dr. Crandon had been visiting and as they were sitting in chairs about the room they suddenly heard Walter's voice....*"Hello, Henry! Think I'm dead, do you?"* In no time, Dr. Hardwicke fell fast asleep and his wife, Kate, began to talk to Walter about such things as ectoplasm. It was said that Walter took ectoplasm from Dr.

Hardwicke's slumbering body and created a bird, a small sparrow hawk, which was at the top of the piano and then after swooping through the room, finally landed on Kate's right ankle, where it proceeded to claw through her silk stockings and draw blood.

The stories that came from Dr. Hardwicke's home bordered on the absurd. A gargantuan Victorian, with turrets that twisted and turned into the sky, the beautiful Fifty-Seventh Street home became the center point of activity in the city of Niagara Falls. Not too far from the banks of the Niagara River and the original landmark of an ancient fortress, Dr. Hardwicke and his wife made their abode into an assembly hall for those who sought an entrance into another world. Séance circles were held regularly and experiments were constantly in the works to prove that there is no death. It is possible that Dr. Hardwicke stopped practicing as a physician quite early on in order to have more time for the paranormal stage he had set up within his own home.

During the 1920's, magic and daredevil routines were steadily becoming America's most favorite form of entertainment. Even Annie Edson Taylor, Niagara's favorite daredevil and the first woman to survive the trip over Niagara Falls in a barrel, spent the last days of her life as "*a medium*," telling people's fortunes from her apartment on Thomas Street. Harry Houdini, the famed magician and escape artist revealed that he was making over $200,000 a year for his strange work. He had been to Niagara on several occasions. Around 1896, he appeared at the old Lyceum Theater on Main Street where he performed his straight jacket and manacle routine to a packed house. By 1921, the temperamental magician came to Niagara, yet again, to film a movie for the Houdini Picture Corporation. People had hoped he would perform amazing and daring stunts at Niagara. Instead, from the Prospect House Hotel, he told reporters that he had been warned by the police that he would be promptly arrested if he attempted any such thing. He admitted that he was not in Niagara to "*flirt with the Fates.*" By 1923, Houdini's moving picture, "*The Man From Beyond,*" was showing at the Bellevue Theatre in Niagara Falls. In the movie, Houdini's character re-emerges from a block of ice and falls in love with his girlfriends' descendant. In the most famous scene, filmed during his stay at Niagara Falls, he swims perilously close to the brink of the falls as he saves the heroine, Nita Naldi, from certain death. And it was noted that he had, indeed, swum perilously close to the brink of the falls while making this movie. Obviously, what he had said to the reporters at the Prospect House in 1921 had been only partly true.

As popular as Houdini was, it was no secret that Dr. Hardwicke had nothing but contempt for him. Greatly interested in Spiritualism following the death of his beloved mother, Houdini's later years were spent furiously debunking fraudulent mediums. He traveled the globe uncovering wicked schemes, yet in the end there was no one who haunted him quite so much as the lovely Mina Crandon. Beautiful, intelligent, Mina would greet her visitors in a flimsy nightgown and silk stockings…attire which left very little to the imagination and bewitched many of the men. She made no financial gain from her gatherings. She was an enigma to many, especially Houdini, and quite possibly to Dr. Hardwicke, as well. She was pursued on every level; by men, women, Spiritualists, fans and by enemies alike.

"You want to know what it feels like to be a witch? You know that's what they would have called me in Boston 150 years ago. And they would have hauled me before the General Court and executed me for consorting with the devil but now they send committees of Professors from Harvard to study me. That represents progress, doesn't it?"

All attempts to debunk her had been countered successfully and she was often considered to be the most extraordinary medium in the world. She had her supporters and they were the most influential names in the field. Sir Arthur Conan Doyle, the well-known author of the Sherlock Holmes mysteries, became deeply involved in Spiritualism following the death of his son in World War I, and was one of her most enthusiastic proponents. It was Conan Doyle who had recommended her to enter a $2,500 contest to prove her psychic ability to the *Scientific American* and it was this action that introduced Mina to Houdini, one of the judges.

Houdini found himself completely stumped, though he believed her to be the slickest ruse he had ever encountered. He stopped at nothing to prove she was a fraud though over and over again he was unable to prove it. In 1924, he created a special "*Anti-Medium's*" cabinet in order to infringe upon all of her body's movements so that there would be no possible way for her to commit any sort of false moves. Houdini, himself, held onto one of her hands while his assistant held her other. Walter exclaimed suddenly that Houdini had meddled with the bell-box and upon investigation there was indeed an item inserted so as to make it difficult to have the bell ring (an exercise that Walter would accomplish during a sitting).

The next occasion involving Houdini and Mina involved Walter, again, communicating that Houdini had attempted once more to tamper with the investigation by placing a rule within the cabinet. Houdini denied it yet he would have been the only one with access to the area. Years later, Houdini's assistant, Jimmy Collins, actually admitted to having been directed by his boss to secretly sabotage the investigation. "*I chucked it in the box myself. The Boss told me to do it. 'E wanted to fix her good.*" Henry Hardwicke proclaimed his own pride in Mina's continued success to a group of Niagara's Spiritualists who met a few years later at the Unitarian Church for a lecture sponsored by the Survival League of America. It was to his great satisfaction that Walter had contemptuously "*showed up Houdini…*"

In the end, the investigators from *Scientific American* denied her the prize she had been seeking, mostly due to Houdini's disagreements. However, Houdini could never actually present proof that she was fraudulent. Although, shortly after, he published an expose of the well -known Boston medium, he "*failed to satisfy those who were looking for final proof, which was, impossible to give because, logically, he couldn't prove a negative— that spiritualism does not exist and that the dead do not survive…*" On

February 11, 1925, *Scientific American* issued their final report which explained that *"...we have observed phenomena the method of production of which we cannot in every case claim to have discovered. But we have observed no phenomena of which we can assert that they could not have been produced by normal means..."*

Houdini died on October 31, 1926, *Halloween*, supposedly from complications of appendicitis. Mina publicly revealed her sorrow at his passing and complimented the tenacity of his attacks upon her, although some ultimately feel she may have had something to do with his death. A few years later, Conan Doyle also died. Mina, who lost much of her credibility after it was found that the wax impressions were not of her brother, Walter's, ghostly thumbprint, but of her dentist's, continued to work at her medium-ship, however from time to time found herself depressed and suicidal, at one occasion leaving a séance and hovering about her roof top where she threatened to jump.

Dr. Hardwicke continued with his work in the spiritual realm and took a job as an instructor at the newly conceived Galahad College in Asheville, North Carolina, in 1932, where he held most of the teaching duties under the infamous founder, William Dudley Pelley. The purpose of the college was *"to overcome a general breakdown in religious conviction; to inspire psychical research; to help combat the menacing crime wave; and to instill the principle of Christ in the American industrial sphere..."* A Fascist, anti-Semite and supporter of Hitler, Pelley used his college as a means of publishing his treatises blending spirituality with right wing extremism. Apparently Pelley's operation was a family affair for Monte Hardwicke, Dr. Henry Hardwicke's son, worked for Pelley, as a printer, along with son-in-law, Daniel Kellogg.

The college was short lived as it was in the midst of the Depression and Pelley was called before the House Un-American Activities Committee and imprisoned until the 1950's. Things had not turned out as planned for the Hardwicke's and on May 11, 1939, only 58 years of age, Dr. Henry Hardwicke was dead. Strangely, Mina Crandon died not too long after, on November 1, 1941, *All Saints Day*, the day that western theology commemorates those who have obtained the beatific vision of heaven.

In the end, they took all of their secrets to their graves.

Interestingly enough, Dr. Hardwicke ends his little book with a scene at Fort Niagara where he wonders about the end of life.

Why does not science, to which the way is now open,--science, that traces the life of the smallest insects through their various stages of existence, show man the answer to his most persistent question?

Whatever the answer, so ends the story of Niagara's, Dr. Henry Hardwicke. Perhaps.

Ghosts

"…and in our turn we too shall pass,

the phantoms of today…"

Colonel Peter A. Porter, unknown

Chapter One
Lovely Place in Winter

There were three men who came with the carriage. Their pockets filled with stones. And there was no such thing as time since if you really think of it—time is a completely made up notion—just a measurement contrived by humans to organize the vast mystical nothingness of the universe. The horses knew about the nothingness of the universe. They had made their way swiftly through the falling snow and in through the black iron gate. They stopped when the driver commanded them to stop and they whinnied and lifted their hooves and scratched and shook their tails of the feathery whitestuff until they were used to the calm of the scene. Yes, of course, they had been here before. They would wait, unfastened, until the men were finished.

One by one the men stepped down from the carriage to begin their task. The driver lit a cigarette, walked around a bit. Stared at the moon. It was midnight, Christmas Eve, and there was a little crack in the organization of the universe. Church bells were sounding nearby while things like snow and men and carriages with horses were seeping in through the open spaces. Mr. Childs, closest to the door, his body bent forward, a silken hat brushing against the doorframe, was the first to exit. He was followed by the newspaperman, Mr. Pool, and the gentle Mr. Clark, Practical Embalmer and Undertaker (and cabinet maker) who knew all about death and dying. They stood in silence for a moment until Pool finally broke open the icy solitude.

--Lovely, lovely place in winter. Isn't it so?

--Yes...Childs whispered.

You might think he was the quiet one (because of the whispering). But, no, you're wrong. He was the one with the busy mind that screamed and kicked wildly behind flickering candle-eyes.

Clark knew this place well. Didn't need to say a single word about the loveliness. Could see the underthings. The worms and the slugs that moved about unhindered in the warm spaces beneath the snow and the grass and the dirt. Little bits of unbroken life swimming among a sea of coffins. The men. The women. The children. All of them with their dusty bodies falling apart bit by bit until one with the wood and the velvet cushions. He imagined seeing so many of their sweet faces for the last time as he closed the lid on their humanity. There they were! One day picking up a book in the library. The next day… gone. So many library books never finished. Sad husbands and wives returning them in their place. Almost looking guilty about the whole affair. Strange thing death is. Hmm…yes…

He let a smile unfold. A secret little smile. One that crept along the side of his frozen lip. Only he could understand. Yes, indeed, it was magnificent to close that lid. Inherently delicious to be the last one to see the curvature of a face. He coughed once into a leather glove as if to say, "Yes, fellows…I know about these things….let me lead you along."

So they moved along in their fine array of overcoats (one being marked down from $10 to a glorious $5.90 at M. Brown's Clothier and Hatter at 106 Falls Street) through the wide expanse of cemetery on this night of nights knowing, one and all, without any sort of announcement, where they were headed and for what business. Very elegant—the three of them dashing through the snow.

--Did you see in the papers? That deer caught in Steuben County? My God…Pure white…imagine that. Wish I'd been there. Didn't say if it was a buck. Probably…would-ah…if it was. Pool lit a cigarette and blew a few smoky rings between his night darkened lips.

Childs was suddenly thrown into the mess of it and perturbed at the thought of the white deer.

--But why capture such a thing? Just let it be, I say. Should-ah let him go. Poor thing. Must-ah been lovely, just lovely. White fur and white snow. Lovely. (He a-hemmed.)

He curled his hands into fists in his pockets. Felt the cold edges of the stones cut into skin. He imagined some nimrod in Steuben County had already killed the poor deer and probably had it hanging on his fiery mantle beside the Christmas tree for all to come at gawk at. Twinkling Christmas lights. Probably Christmas carols being sung…Once Again…Father Lead Me…Tours Te Deum…surely not as lovely as that sung on Christmas Eve at the First Presbyterian…but nonetheless… family gathered. Blood stains on white. Dripping onto carpets.

No one said any more about the deer. But still Childs could not push it out of that corner it had taken up in his mind.

They continued near the front of Oakwood, ever mindful of their work. Now below the beautiful angel. The sullen angel. Arms crossed in supplication. Head bowed. Carefully carved stone folds of holy robe. All pinned together by a stone mason. Maybe an Italian with loving hands. Here they placed their first piles of stones. Utter silence and the structure of the stones and the angel glaring down at them reminded Pool of art so it was then that he mentioned Cameron's painting, *Niagara Falls in Winter*.

--Bought by some HH Warner of Rochester…purchasing price $30,000! Imagine that.…

--No, couldn't be.

Clark shook his head and imagined 30,000 pieces of anything at all. Slugs crawling (earth sticking to their bellies), squirrels, twigs, dead leaves, specks of dirt, flakes of snow. Just couldn't be possible.

--But it's true!

--And they say it's regarded as the finest landscape ever painted in America, said Childs with pride.

They all had seen it. Had even seen Peter Caledon Cameron. A colossal work, it was, this *Niagara Falls in Winter*. Like the falls, perhaps. Well, not quite…But it was one of the ones that let you hear the thunder and feel the spray on your face when you stood before it.

--Good perspective he had...ha! Pool added. His heavy boots crunching along. More smoke rings from his mouth to the sky.

Then they spoke of how Mr. Cameron had painted his studies of Niagara Falls from a point in mid-air. Had lowered himself down the precipice with a tackle.

--A lot of guts these artists have...one standing for hours on end until the icicles formed on his beard...

--Pure mania, said Clark.

Indeed, they all knew the maniacs Niagara had summoned year after year.

--Yes, quite so, said Childs, concurring with both the "guts" statement as well as the "mania" statement.

--There are some things that bring you to your knees, he thought to himself. Some things.

Their voices went on as their thoughts became more unbearable and heavy to carry. They filled the horrid blackness of the night with half laughs, coughs, with the clearing of throats. Of course, the moving on made it inevitable that they would soon pass over their wives' graves, their children's graves, their own graves. Probably the reason for all the small talk and nervousness. But how strange to be on this side of the whole thing! There was a cold pause upon coming nearer to these tender spots of earth filled with salty tears and their loved ones bodies. Childs passed beside the little one... "We'll miss him when there is noble work to do..." Son, Joel. Reduced to an etching on some stone. 45ᵗʰRegiment Illinois Volunteers. Died Battle of Shiloh. That's it, though. There was nothing more. All comes to this.

They came. They saw. They placed the stones--for they were the most diligent of men. Never give up the ship, these ones. Even some stones for the dreary Woolson graves—that strange set from Pool's own family. A family of horrible circumstances. Tragic ends.

Flashes of newsprint. Poison. Blood. Murder. Suicide. May they rest in peace. Requiescat in pace.

Then onto Strangers Rest (for they need the stones the most). Those forgotten travelers and the lost. A little pile of stones mean the most to those left behind. Keeps them going. The tragic ones who had no names or whose names had faded from every ledger. Those too young to hold a pencil. Those without a hand. Come back from the War, pieces missing. Those with only hands. Found in the River. Just a limb with a tattoo. Annie. Stones for all of them. Little calling cards.

Almost time to go. Things are closing up. The three men have emptied their pockets. The horses know about the nothingness of the universe. About the nothingness of Time. They whinny, scratch, shake their manes of snowflakes. Almost. Time. To. Go. So short these visits. But there are other things to do. They make their way back to the carriage. The driver never says a single word. In they go. Pool puts out his cigarette, the light is gone. He is the first to lower his head, climb in. He is followed by Clark and Childs. Solemn work. Not so bad but, indeed, solemn work. Just the remembering that there is an end is the toughest part. There are always other beginnings. But there is always an end.

The driver shuts the door, steps into his seat, calls to the horses. Sleigh bells ring, are you listening? One more stop for this night of all nights. The store of Louis Ehrig is always open if you believe Time is a made up notion. It is crowded with people. Frontier Mart. Falls Street. The attraction? A great Christmas tree trimmed in the most beautiful manner. Lighted wax candles on every branch. Mr. Ehrig proclaimed this evening that this IS the headquarters of Santa Claus. It's December 24, 1855. It always is December 24, 1855, and the store is full to capacity. A carriage is on its way. Pockets full of money for gifts. Three men exit the carriage for Santa's headquarters. Their children can hardly wait. Tomorrow is Christmas morning.

Chapter Two

A Little Ghost Story to Commemorate the Life and Death (and the reawakening) of Captain Matthew Webb

Perhaps she was a raving lunatic, or perhaps she had actually spoken with him many years following his death in Niagara's rapids. We will never know for sure. We do know a few things, though...that in May of 1893 a party of travelers stopped here at Niagara Falls on their way to the World's Fair. They were with the Polytechnic Cooperative Excursion Co. of No. 309 Regent Street, London, England—a peculiar bunch led by Mr. Newton Smith. Their group included a somnambulist who kept the whole ship from sleeping and another woman, Miss Hall, who combined vegetarianism and spiritualism and stirred it all up with a *"cranky disposition."* We also know that Miss Hall, or *"Snowdrop,"* as she was known in the spirit realm, claimed to have had an encounter with the ghost of Captain Matthew Webb, the champion swimmer who had broken all records by successfully swimming the English Channel in 1875 but lost his life to Niagara on July 24, 1883.

But then there was poor Miss Ettie Castle, of London, England! Unfortunately, she had the misfortune of sharing a room on board the steamship with the sleep walker and the vegetarian-spiritualist. It was anything but smooth sailing as she was repeatedly awakened throughout the night by the startling cries of Miss Hall who was convinced that she was being pursued by demons and by the other strange woman who *"got in her work"* and wandered around the cabin as if in a trance. It seemed inevitable that a visit to Niagara would incite more fantastic supernatural events. One of the most vibrant cities in the world for spiritualists, the falling water was believed to fascinate one and all. So it was no surprise that Miss Hall found herself in the midst of another realm while gazing upon the rapids and the whirlpool. She revealed afterward that it was here *in this place* that a fine gentleman came upon her and struck up a melancholy conversation. He was handsome, friendly... and his very presence commanded respect. An Englishwoman, she knew at once it was him. During Victorian times Captain Webb's face was well known throughout the British Empire. It was not uncommon for the traveler to pay a visit to his grave at Oakwood Cemetery. But here he stood before her, at the scene of his demise, just a shadow of a man...but still a man, nonetheless, and he lamented his sad state of affairs.

"*Snowdrop...I regret that I took that last trip. It was a little too much for me that time and I should not have tried it.*"

Miss Hall claimed that these were his exact words.

Though he was king of the world for a time after his miraculous conquering of the English Channel in twenty one hours and forty five minutes (back in 1875), his brazen idea of beating Niagara was never a good one. He received no encouragement from the locals who knew that only tragedy would come of this sort of sport. It didn't matter to them that he was a superstar. He had no chance against Niagara. When the date of his planned swim arrived--Tuesday, July 24th, 1883-- it was said he was cheerful and perfectly confident of impending success. He left the Clifton House at about 4:00 and walked down a hill where he took a small scow and was rowed out into the river while an audience of onlookers gathered to watch the spectacle. He was never seen again after 4:33 that summer afternoon.

All that was left was to wait for Niagara to spit out his body—which occurred in Lewiston on Saturday, July 28th. A telegram was sent to Boston at once to inform his wife of the sad occurrence. Coroner Elsheimer took the body under his care and finally it was sent on to Oakwood Cemetery to remain in the vault for many months until Mrs. Webb could decide the next course of action. A "*very incomplete postmortem examination*" was made and it was revealed that he had been killed by the intense pressure of the water. Ultimately, Mrs. Webb decided to leave him to us, to Niagara. The casket was trimmed with Masonic emblems and members of the local fraternity assisted with the burial in the midst of a severe winter storm and deep snow.

Did Mrs. Webb err upon leaving him here, lonesome, at Niagara-the final tragic scene of a great life? Perhaps the Captain doesn't appreciate living in the shadow of his defeat for at night it is still possible to hear Niagara's great heaving roar through the cars and people-noises. Maybe it's time for us to make an effort to take notice--like the raving vegetarian-spiritualist, Miss Hall-- when we hear those little whispers from the past. It could awaken something very interesting, like Captain Matthew Webb, himself.

Chapter Three

Another Homeless Ghost; An imaginary encounter with Mrs. Mary Anna Laughlin Walker

It was a Sunday in August following the destruction of the house known as *"921 Main Street"* when I met with a ghost in Oakwood Cemetery. Out of the corner of my eye, I was sure that I could see a weeping and agitated female form lingering over a distant gravestone. She had appeared out of summer rain and nothingness. I suddenly thought for a moment that she must be an incarnation of what my friend would call a *lepke*; a perfect and human manifestation in a cemetery, undeniably visible for a short time. And then she was gone. But before her inscrutable disappearance I walked over to her and spoke with her. She, being fascinated by this acknowledgement of her being, told me about herself and how the demolition of her home rendered her a homeless ghost. How she, and so many of our other pioneers who have found themselves forced out of their living quarters, are lost in Niagara…and what would I do? I told her that I was not a wrangler of ghosts, but I would listen to her story and do my best to render assistance.

Our little tryst began with me seated under a shady oak, pencil and paper in hand, and with her draped over a tall gravestone, elbows bent and a fist beneath a pointy chin. Her dress was white and impeccably pressed. Her eyes unfolded before me as if a giant blue banner, not unlike the sky and clouds. A little breeze picked up and I noticed how—unnaturally-- her hair did not move as mine did. She appeared *other*-dimensional and fixed as a movie image—although I understood that she was actually alive (in some sense) and that she eerily contemplated all of my moves with great interest.

Feverishly, she began to relay the week's horrible events, but not without telling me the details of her life and the circumstances of her spiritual disarray. Her voice was faint, a passing whimper, and as I scribbled furiously I am sure I missed bits and pieces while an ambulance or a helicopter flooded the soundscape. And so she commenced her story with the tragic events of August 4, 2011…

Being afflicted so regularly with the usual weakness and dissipation that comes from the break of day and sunlight…I wondered what noise and commotion had stirred me from that heavy sleep. It was the men and their machines coming for my house. I was much familiar with that sense of impending violence toward that vessel of my being. There had been talk before of destruction and in years past even fires had swept through this place. I slammed doors and shrieked with a voice to the center of my energy source--but to no avail. I was taken for the wind. As for the fire...I had been able to stop it before it consumed the place. Whirling like a cyclone. Blowing into the burning cinders with a deep and cold breath. I saved some paintings that way....But this time it was...unstoppable...their rude machines clawing into the veins within the walls, tearing through layers and stairwells, ripping away the rooftop. Terror accosted me and I found myself clinging to pieces of wood, a floorboard, a doorframe...shrinking into a spider's web. Then the great and formidable quiet...and the questions that plagued me most of all. What to do? Where will I go? This house had been my shelter for many years. Of course, Anthony had wanted me out and now he has finally had his day...but I will have mine yet....

Her eyes blackened with this and turned away from me, for a moment, and then she began again.

I surveyed the scene and bounced onto the warmth of a passerby. He was kindly, though very perturbed at my home's wreckage. Almost as if it had been his own. And then he took a piece of the rubble and carried it off. It was the "921" and it was a piece of my home. Miserable and defeated, I curled in between the numbers until I fell asleep. When I awakened...I found that I was here....at this place. And I was not alone. There are others here that have found themselves in a similar predicament...their ancient haunts desecrated to a pile of rubble. We wander together and alone. We take turns gathering heat from the living, from rays of sun, from squirrels and rabbits, the crows...from you. And your heat gives us form and voice.

It was then that she extended a bony, white hand and brought it to my cheek and my thoughts rushed away in a tumble of water as wild as Niagara Falls. I was frightened to the depths of my soul but, still, there was a curiosity that stopped me from running out of those gates. Though I trembled, I couldn't help but ask her...*who are you?* And she answered...

My name is Mary Anna Walker. Ha...I had almost forgotten that I had a name as it has been ages since I have told anyone at all. Or heard it uttered...When I was a girl...I was Mary Anna Laughlin. I was born in 1862, in the old village of LaSalle. My people were Irish Catholics. I remember most...the peaches. The most wonderful peaches in the world grew on Cayuga Island. Everyone would come for them. If only I could taste one now...it was the peaches that brought him to me, my Anthony. We courted for a short time. Our pleasure was to race with his team alongside the river with our hearts on fire. How Niagara will do that to you...make you wish to join her in that rush over the rocks. Into her cool, sweet mouth. We were married in 1878. He was from Suspension Bridge, then Clarksville, the son of English Protestants. Just the beginning of our troubles...

And our Mary cried. It was strange for me to see a ghost with actual tears and I contemplated that fact but then reassured myself that the whole experience was unlike any other. I wasn't sure if she had decided she had said enough and just as I was on the verge of disappointment she spoke again...

It was a life of luxury...my little stint as Miss-us An-tho-ny Walk-er. He was an entrepreneur even at seventeen. Let me tell you he held the sole proprietorship of the laundry industry in Niagara Falls for many years. With a four cylinder mangle that cost more than $1,000...he could do flat work and his plant had a capacity of 9,000 pieces per day. Not to mention a Sinclair shirt ironer and a Durey shirt starcher. The boiler had a 60 horsepower capacity. Lots of steam! Mr. Walker had plenty of steam and some to share! Hahaha...

And she laughed but it really wasn't so much of a laugh as it was a mockery of a laugh. It was frightening and made me gasp for breath to hear the ghost laugh like this.

"Fine work done, Mr. Walker! A laundry and carpet cleaning establishment that is a credit to the city of Niagara Falls! Everything done in No. 1 order. Tip top. Ship shape. Family Washing 4 cents a pound. No. 356, No. 358 and No. 360 Main Street...telephone is 46..."

She smoothed her sleeves, the perfect lines of her skirt. Pushed her face so close into mine that I caught a fluttering aroma...one of wet leaves and grass, dirt, the ruffled feathers of a black bird.

And such a fleet of swift carriages he had...delivering the fruits of his sanitary enterprise throughout the day hours. But it was the night that was for soiling those perfect white sheets...with his filthy girlfriends. When my boy was just a little molly-coddle, he stayed closer to home...and it was our amiable Nancy Young—servant girl—a Canuck-- that brought a glimmer to his eye. I was sorely forgotten and stashed away like the fine china...only brought out when necessary. He certainly ate off the other little plates...Miss Margy Hayes and Miss Clara Jackson...and in the end didn't his sweethearts receive all the leftovers? For me, the crumbs...one dollar, Miss Pencil-pusher. How would you feel about one dollar for a lifetime of servitude and devotion?

I let go of my pencil and set my paper on the grass. Miss Pencil-pusher! Of course, I was confused and frightened by her pathos. She was quite assuredly, a woman rejected and scorned for ages. What pent up sadness! She was one of those lost souls; expected to *"put up"* with much more than the rest of us. And when she told me about Howard James, I felt it would have been rude for me to start writing again, so I made mental note of the rest of our encounter.

Howard James was born in September of 1889 and I lost him on February 25, 1914. He was only twenty five and just two years into his marriage with Florence upon his death. They were married in Welland in order to evade such publicity as would have followed him. Of course, there was that other marriage...but it hadn't worked out. I suppose like father, like son...In the end all that really mattered was that it wasn't fair that a woman could lose everything she ever had. I had my social and civic affairs and my circle of friends...but that wasn't enough for a woman who had lost a husband and a child. And then...my home.

Anthony died on March 18, 1921, leaving a large estate and a very peculiar will. To his former employee, the constant Margy Hayes, bookkeeper— $10,000, a house and a lot in Ontario. To his tried and true Miss Clara Jackson- -$5,000 and an island in the Niagara! St. Mary's Hospital received a $4,000 *legacy. For Mrs. Anthony Walker? Hahaha...$1.00. If it weren't for the swift business of Judge Hickey it would have been $1.00 and $1.00 alone...but his reconstruction of the will gave me life use of the homestead at 921 Main Street. That was it and I vowed I would never leave. Never ever leave 921 Main Street.*

She stopped and walked a few paces; propped herself, like a doll, against her little gravestone...*Mary A. Walker, 1862-1938.* She was pensive, deep in thought for a moment, and then she shook her head gracefully and concluded her story.

But I've left 921 Main Street, now haven't I? In fact, it was really a prison, wasn't it? Your friend carried me away in his arms. I must have been quite the burden. I do hope he didn't receive any slivers or blisters from the cracked and broken wood. My ridiculous green and purple painted beauty! But he saved me and he saved my "921." Like a sea captain, he took me through a bumpy mysterious expanse of time and destiny, and now I'm here...where I belong...in Oakwood. Howard is here, and Anthony...yes, there is much, much time for reconciliation...or not. It's up to me what I want...after all of these years. I am waiting for a crow or a person, maybe a child full of vibrance, to walk through these gates and give them some light so we can begin again. I have seen the others, the shadows, the homeless ghosts who have been cast out into the darkness and the cold but have somehow made it here...and they wait for you. Always wait and then take a little piece of your light...just a little piece is all we need to come alive.

I picked up my pencil and my paper to write some more, but our supposed *"lepke"* was gone and instead a large black crow stood and shook out its rain soaked wings upon the grave of Mary Anna Walker. Somehow, I had the feeling that I would see her one day, again, soon. And I was tired, very tired.

Death Sketches

"Still with sad heart his requiem pour

amid the cataract's ceaseless roar…"

Lydia Sigourney, 1834

Chapter One

A Dreadful End;

Elmira Millard

During the mid-19ᵗʰ century the newspapers were full of tales of suicide and death in the Niagara River. Most involved unrequited love and romanticized tales of misfortune and catastrophe. One of the more obscure stories was of a young girl who was destined for tragedy.

Elmira Millard was not like the other girls. Although as beautiful as she was pure and as she was sought after by many young men, she never had a lover—for she preferred not one. In fact, her dearest friend related many years later that Elmira would often say: *I am only in love with myself.* She spent her days in a sort of narcissistic self-embrace shunning any chances of sharing herself with another. Perhaps she was well aware of her *strange affliction.*

It was a hot summer's day in the mid-1800's when a little, dried-up peculiar looking old German made his way up the steps of her porch. At once making himself at home, he asked if he might have a seat and a cold drink. She kindly obliged but couldn't help notice how he gazed deeply into her eyes with a burning obsession. Finally he revealed that he was a fortune teller and it was not by accident that he had ventured into her presence. Curious as to her fortune, she allowed him to take her hand. It was remarkable how much he was able to divulge of past occurrences from her life's story! She sat in amazement. But as he continued his words became increasingly dark. Perhaps much of what he revealed was not a surprise. He told her that she had been born unlucky, and that she was destined to bring evil upon all who loved her. He went on to add, "...*those from whom you receive presents and those to whom you give them will die...and the stars predict for you a dreadful end in the near future...*" Poor Elmira was stunned beyond belief and from that day forward found herself in a cloud of doom. She brooded over his fateful words and as much as her friend tried to cheer her spirits she was unable to lift herself from her depression.

And in the end, the fortune teller's tale of woe was fulfilled. Exactly four weeks following his prediction she was found drowned in the Niagara River. It was believed that she had gone into the rapids above the falls and had been carried off to a watery grave.

Chapter Two

Forgotten Sleeps;
Emily Helena Lodge

No doubt a woman who had spent so much of her life on water, Emily must have reveled at the sheer force that met her at the brink of the falls as it rushed headlong into that boiling soup of white foam and rainbow. To most everyone—that first sighting instills feelings of fear and awe followed by a deep reverence. The Native Americans called it the abode of Henu, thunder god, and legends reveal stories of sacrifice and appeasement. Henu was always hungry for a sparkling woman and it was said beautiful maidens were often sent over in birch boats to momentarily quell his insatiable desires. Residents continue to insist that Henu never ceases to claim at least four souls each year.

Mr. F. W. Lodge and wife had found close quarters in Room 27 at the Cataract House. The Cataract was magnificent in its day. *"Enormous…yet very comfortable…,"* one 19th century woman found she *"would often lose (her) way in it…"* Prominent people from all walks of life, including historical figures such as Abraham Lincoln and General Stonewall Jackson had taken lodging at the beautiful hotel that had overlooked the American rapids—every waking moment an earthquake of sorts. Samuel DeVeaux had written in one of the earliest guide books that travelers not accustomed to the sounds would often awaken in the night imagining themselves *"in the midst of a tempest."* Those who had the special pleasure of taking a room in a wing that stretched out over the rapids remarked that the noise was such that they *"could not even hear themselves speak."* I wonder when her head fell against her pillow, did she know she was at the edge of the world?

"My dreams are wild here. I am not calm. A great voice seems calling on me, which I am too feeble to answer."

Emily's death was not remarkable. A most typical passage she died of natural causes just a few days after her husband signed the register at the Cataract House. Bilious fever had ravaged her young body, left her for dead, put an abrupt end to a romantic journey. It was common knowledge that *"jaundice (was) going here"* in October of 1864. Suffering violent pain in the head, unpleasant sensation in the stomach, chill, flushes of heat, irregular pulse, nausea, accompanied by a most copious evacuation of bile and jaundice—Mr. F.W. Lodge's wife slipped away in her room at the Cataract House. It was a quiet parting. She had no family in the vicinity and it had been too short a visit to have made many friends.

Miss Frances Monck, another guest at the Cataract House that week jotted hastily in her diary that *"a lady had died in the hotel this morning,"* but briskly went on to other things such as what a *"lovely and fine day"* it truly was. The whole thing did not stir much pity in this city still deep in mourning from the loss of so many lives just a few months before on a battlefield in Cold Harbor, Virginia. In fact, as if to add insult to injury, even poor little Letitia Porter, only daughter of the late hero of the Battle at Cold Harbor, Colonel Peter A. Porter, and Mrs. Porter, was buried that very week in a freak hail storm that swept through Niagara Falls with heavy thunder and lightning leaving a blanket of pure white ground cover. So far from home in a country embroiled in civil war, it was destined that Emily would stay in Niagara. Her grief stricken husband had illustrious plans for honoring her final resting place, however, it seems the respectful doctor, W.O. Davis, whom he had left a large sum of money with, never actually found a way to allow them to fully materialize. Letters that remain in a collection held by the Lodge family dated December 24, 1864, and May 15, 1867, reveal a husband's frustration and a litany of various obstacles: a workman's strike, a shortage of the requested materials, frozen ground. There were plans for a great monument with posts and a roof, a special unique shade of marble, a rail and chains. The amount of money mentioned would have a modern value of almost $3,000. Most likely, Dr. Davis erected an inferior stone and pocketed most of the remaining money—imagining Emily's husband would never return to the area. And who would ever realize the inadequacy? We do know that over one hundred and forty years later, no evidence of the magnificent resting place is visible at Lot #366. Assigned to a Mr. Frederic C. Lodge (possibly a misrepresentation of Francis W. Lodge's name or signature), the lot went up for auction in 1943, after the family failed to claim it, and the plot was subdivided. Emily and her grave faded into oblivion. Or so it seemed....

It's a strange thing, but there is something about Emily that refuses to go away. In August of 1891, someone happened to visit the site of a grave marked:

Emily Helena

Daughter of Major Crummer

Late of HRH 25th Regt. and Wife of Francis W. Lodge

The visitor went so far as to scratch out a poem and publish it in the Niagara Falls Gazette, forever immortalizing one woman, Emily Helena Crummer Lodge, whom the author had claimed had died *"many years ago at the Cataract House."*

"Her grave, with spreading briar is grown,

And most the name o'er wends,

Upon the shattered fallen stone,

That tells of home and friends;

Are British hearts, so hard and cold,

And dead to Love's bequest,

That Valor's child forgotten sleeps,

In Strangers' Rest?

O, Roll Niagara's mighty wave,

Sing to her in her dreams,

With tears of spray bedew her grave,

And sunlight flood with beams,

O, birds at morn sing sweetly there,

Beside your happy rest,

And stars of night look kindly down,

In Strangers' Rest."

For the longest time we were unsure of the exact location of Emily's grave. The situation was intriguing and we knew that according to the description she had been sleeping beneath earth and sky in Strangers (or Travelers Rest) for many, many years. Today, Strangers Rest is the neat little triangle toward the back of the cemetery.

In Emily's midst are other strangers and travelers to Niagara. Some had no family, others had no name. Many had taken the plunge over the edge of the world. Others had lost all identity after having been bashed and obliterated by rocks and currents. Here lie violent ends. Lonely, single graves. The stunters and daredevils. Pretty little rows of children. Many are unmarked; no monument ever erected. Uncared for, many have been covered by a natural layer of grass, moss and brush. Here lies a playground for the imagination, a grove of unfinished stories. In times past, it was not uncommon for lady travelers, perhaps not unlike the author of Emily's poem, to stop and place flowers at these tragic, lonesome graves, for they knew they stood in a strange intersection between heaven and earth.

Again, it was seemingly a perfect accident that enabled us to eventually find the exact location of Emily's grave. We had searched throughout that triangular area for months. Record of her burial did not exist within the ledger books for 1864, though we knew from the poem and from the death notice listed in the *Sydney Morning Herald* that on October 10, 1864, Emily Helena had died at Niagara Falls. It all seemed too right to be wrong. As a result, without an accurate reference point, we were on a seemingly perpetual quest for the needle in the haystack. We used prods and shovels, dowsing rods, maps and transcribed letters as guides. We called in the experts, found descendants from Australia and California, psychics and a team of investigators from NF Paranormal. Although it seemed a fruitless search—it became apparent that an amazing phenomenon was taking place. The desire to discover Emily's whereabouts had become a literal obsession. This one woman who had died in obscurity was creating quite an uproar. And then one Sunday morning it happened.

Pete had arrived earlier than usual in order to find a spot in the cemetery where a young man, Charles Crysler, had committed a terrible act of despair by taking his own life over the top of his mother's grave, in July of 1891—ironically, one month before the poem to Emily appeared in the Niagara Falls Gazette. As the young man's stone-- like Emily's-- seemed reclusive, Pete decided to canvas the general area. Although he did not find the marker to commemorate his gravesite, he instead found himself face to face with another remarkable stone beside a large pine tree. Visibly aged and broken perfectly in half, though carefully fastened and replaced upon a base, this gravestone was marble with a rounded top. Some illegible carvings, a symbol inside an oval and two words glanced back up at him: *Emily Helena*. At first he was unsure if this was actually *our Emily*, as this location is not within the boundaries of present day Strangers Rest, though very close. But upon a quick flip through the 20,000 lot records in Oakwood Cemetery, he was able to find the notation for Lot #366. The burial record states that grave #1 holds *"Emily H. Lodge."* It had to be her.

Emily's story began on March 26th, 1828 on the Homeric island of Corfu, off the western coast of Greece. It was said that her father, Major James Henry Crummer, a seasoned veteran of the Napoleonic Wars and commandant of the British forces at Kalamos, had fallen madly in love with a beautiful young Greek refugee and had spared no time in taking her for his own. They were married at the residence of the Lord High Commissioner of Corfu on the island of Kalamos. He was 30 years old and she was only 16. But Aikaterina Plessos was hardly just another young Greek refugee girl. It was true that this line of mothers and daughters were more goddess than woman. The island of Corfu had been made for love. Popular legend reveals that Poseidon, god of the sea, had fallen in love with the nymph, Korkyra, daughter of the river god, Aesopus. He kidnapped her and brought her to one of the most beautiful places on earth, a small and unnamed paradise off the west coast of Greece. On this place, also known as the Emerald Island, the waters are crystal clear, the beaches white, multitudes of vibrant flowers dot the landscape. Poseidon honored his new captive-bride by naming this paradise for her, Korkyra (the Greek name for Corfu).

As if following a mythical pattern, Emily's grandmother, Vasiliki, was so devastatingly beautiful that a Turkish pasha named Moukhtar, son of Ali Pasha, abducted her and brought her to live in his harem near Ioannina. Aikaterina spent her early years in this harem until she, too, caught the eye of various powerful men. At the age of 12 she was arranged in marriage to Dr. Iannis Kolettis. He broke off the engagement when the Pasha was executed for revolting against the Sultan and went on to become a prime minister of the Hellenic Republic.

But Aikaterina's brush with history did not end with Dr. Kolettis. Homeless, she found herself living with an uncle in Mesolonghi—an ancient city at the entrance to the Gulf of Corinth. It was here, in 1821, that she repeatedly met with Lord Byron before he died of malaria while fighting for Greek independence from the Turks. At her death she was publicized as *"Byron's Last Friend"* and it was well known that she had never forgotten the minutest details of her acquaintance with one of the world's most beloved poets.

Following Byron's death and the Turkish blockade of Mesolonghi, Aikaterina found herself a refugee on the island of

Kalamos. Mostly women and children, 100,000 in number, a British army detachment was stationed here as part of the occupation of the Ionian Islands. It was commanded by Captain J.H. Crummer. Ultimately for Aikaterina, It, too, was a man who emerged from the sea to sweep her away. This time Poseidon wore a British army officer's coat and took his bride to a different Emerald Island, Ireland, and then across the world to settle a new continent called Australia.

Before leaving for Ireland in 1829, Katherine (her name now Anglicized) gave birth to twin girls on the island of Corfu. Only Emilia survived. Poor Helena did not. However, sometime later Emily took the name of her lost sister and set it beside her own. The children kept coming for Captain Crummer and his wife. Katherine, just a young girl herself, had become pregnant, yet again, with twins who are said to have been born in Ireland, the birthplace of their father. And so huddled in her mother's arms Emily left her birth country and began a life of sea and seamen, of water and sky.

On May 22, 1835, James H. Crummer, Captain of the ship, *England*, left the port of London with his family and the 28th Regiment of Foot and headed for Sydney, New South Wales, Australia. The journey lasted over four months' time. Finally, on October 6, they arrived at their destination. Emily, only seven years old, her mother, her brother, Robert Sherer, and her sister, Eliza Bettina, made history on this day as they became the very first non-convict Greeks to settle in this area. Appointed Police Magistrate on June 8, 1836, and Commander of the Iron Gang, Captain Crummer brought his family to live in Newcastle.

This strange new land on the other side of the world was full of opportunity but the idea of living here may have been not just a little frightening for Mrs. Crummer. Previously known as a *"hell hole of dangerous convicts,"* Newcastle's penal colony period had ended just a decade before. As if it wasn't bad enough that Australia was founded as a convict settlement, Newcastle had an even worse reputation as being the outpost for repeat offenders. Harsh, hot and dry, surrounded by rugged unexplored land, crawling with unfriendly tribes of aborigines and even (the rumor of) cannibals, this place had only been accessible by water and intrepid seamen until the completion of the Great Northern Road in 1836—one built with the sweat and blood of thousands of men in leg irons. Completed by convicts and still in use today, this road opened the area up to settlers. Convicts also made up the servant population of Newcastle. In fact, various criminals were employed at the Crummer household. Their antics have been chronicled in the local newspapers of the period. It was here in this strange brew of characters and geography, of runaway sailors, convicts and wild lands that Miss Emily Crummer came to womanhood.

These unusual experiences did not deter the quickly growing Crummer family. The captain became a major on July 27, 1839, and Emily welcomed numerous additional siblings. Unfortunately, the 19th century was a time in which children barely ever outlived their parents due to the prevalence of childhood illnesses. The Crummer family was not immune to this and it was said in Katherine's obituary that she had outlived all but two of her eleven children.

It is not difficult to imagine the sadness that must have filled much of their time in New South Wales. The death notices in the *Sydney Gazette* and *New South Wales Advertiser* tell a grim tale for sure. Even the Major mentions in a speech to the chairman and gentlemen present at his farewell dinner at Mr. James Hannell's, *Ship Inn*, on the 4th of October, 1849, that he had lived "*fourteen years here, my daughter married here and one of my daughters buried here…*"

The *daughter buried* was possibly thirteen year old Juliana, who had passed away just a few months before. The *daughter married* was most certainly Emily, for she had been married at Christ Church, Newcastle, on June 17, 1848. It was just a few years before that she had been introduced to a handsome young sea captain, Francis Wilkins Lodge.

Once again, following family tradition, it was a man from the sea who had come to steal the heart of one of the Plessos women. More god than man, Captain FW Lodge was well known in these parts. He had begun his seafaring life at the tender age of eight, after having run away from home. The commander of the 480 ton barque, the *Eleanor Lancaster,* Captain Lodge spent his days fearlessly encircling the globe. Commanders were often a *"tough and virile bred of men—romantic and beloved by the public."* Captain Lodge was no exception. A young widower, he had lost his first wife *"suddenly, at sea, on Easter Sunday"* in 1846. He was dashing, full of remarkable energy, courage and wit. The papers of the time remind us that the merchant shipping business was one that was indispensable to the inhabitants of New South Wales. The arrival of a ship such as the *Eleanor Lancaster* meant that there would be fresh shipments of journals of the London news, barrels of tar, brandy, cases of cigars, haberdashery, wine, bales of sheepskin and wool, bags of wheat. Australians, set apart from their European homeland, surely felt that shipmasters such as Lodge were the lifeline to the civilized world, the first path toward communication in the darkness. Sir Oliver Joseph Lodge, physicist, writer and Spiritualist, as well as the nephew of Captain Lodge, wrote in his autobiography that his uncle Frank had *"a hard and adventurous life…was a striking man…his talks were innumerable…a(n) energetic man…"* It was said that Captain Lodge had earned the trust of his contemporaries—and this had *"brought him a certain amount of fame in shipping circles…"*

Various authors have attempted to study the type of women who lived this strange and exciting life. The 1800's was a period of great circumnavigating of the globe. Millions of people moved about as they uprooted themselves from their ancestral locations and found new homes in unexplored areas of the world. Emily fit neatly into this category as she had traveled over the seas as the daughter of an army captain. She was no stranger to the sea and the life of a traveler. Interestingly enough, the sea captain's wife was often a breed of her own. She was fashionable, brave and smart. Most spent their time sewing, reading, writing, practicing navigation and studying languages.

In fact there was a special *Loan Library for Seamen* in New York which provided reading materials for sailing vessels. Many wives kept diaries, however, at this time it is unknown if Emily had kept one--therefore we must infer from other sources as to what this part of her life was like.

We do know that just one month after signing the marriage registry at Christ Church with a capricious signature that ran beyond her husband's and father's... Emily was off at sea. According to the *Shipping Intelligence* published in the Sydney Morning Herald, their honeymoon voyage had been to Auckland, New Zealand. It was in the midst of a southern hemisphere winter when Captain and Mrs. Lodge approached this newly settled land, probably bringing supplies to former British soldiers and their families who were now inhabiting this island. Perhaps they spent some time there, away from family, on the sparkling water of the Waitemata Harbour, where they celebrated this new life as sea captain and wife. Of course, there was always work to be done and according to the captain's nephew, Sir Oliver Lodge, all of his uncles seemed "*to live for work, rather than for sport of any kind...*" But the mornings in Auckland are unlike any other place in the world. There is a well-known saying that reveals the fact that in all seasons on this island paradise, the great beauty of the day is in the morning. A traveler, he must have noticed...*a solemn stillness holds, and a perfect calm prevails.* It was the morning of their life together and night seemed far away.

By October 15th, they were off again, this time just a short trip to Adelaide. It is interesting to note that Emily was indeed on board ship once again. Many wives of sea captains found their honeymoon voyage to be the last journey they would ever make, forever preferring the land to the sea. *Paying homage to Neptune*, or seasickness, was not uncommon. No one was immune. Even the well-seasoned captains and sailors inevitably experienced it at times. Once the seasickness subsided, however, the loneliness and homesickness sank in. It seems that Emily was an exception, though. Whether or not she was homesick or lonely, she continued onward beside her husband and set sail innumerable times to such exotic locations as San Francisco, Honolulu, China and Mexico. One can't help but wonder… did she persist for adventure or for love? Or was it both?

One of the more memorable voyages of the *Eleanor Lancaster* was that fateful journey to San Francisco. The ship was forever immortalized when it left the port of Sydney on January 21, 1849. In what was considered the *"greatest migration since the Crusades,"* over a quarter of a million people came to California in only two years' time. Many of these travelers were from Australia and New Zealand. It was in the midst of the great California Gold Rush, with all accolades to the captain, that the *Eleanor Lancaster* had made it to San Francisco in record time. Arriving in only seventy one days, after making direct passage, she had made it quicker than any other ship. She was, unquestionably, *Queen of the sea.*

After dropping anchor at Benecia, at the mouth of the Sacramento River on April 2, 1849—just a few days after Emily celebrated her twenty-first birthday—the entire crew abandoned ship for the gold fields. Apparently this was not an uncommon occurrence. The San Francisco harbor was a *"perfect forest of masts as far as the eye could reach"* and most of them empty ships. Finding himself in quite a predicament, the Captain unfettered his ship's boats and made a lucrative business of ferrying passengers up or across the river. The route to the diggings from San Francisco was about 160 miles long up the Sacramento. It was said that some paid up to $100 for passage. The captain soon found a way to secure enough of a crew--men who were paid extremely high wages—so that he and Emily could transform the abandoned ship into a store ship, a grog shop and a nursing facility. It has been written that Emily's *"only regret was that she did not have her piano."* It would have made for better business. Piano, or not, this twenty-one year old woman did not keep her fingers idle. And business was booming. There was much work to be done and the captain had no other living soul to depend on but Emily.

San Francisco was wild and lawless while the Lodges were in town. Gangs of ex-convicts and vigilantes wandered the streets. It was dangerous and violent and ultimately *"no paradise to live in."* It seems, however, that business was good for the Captain and his wife. The papers in New South Wales informed their readers that as Captain Lodge was enjoying *"a first rate business"* he had made up his mind to stay in San Francisco for some time. They further explained that the *"attraction must be inviting."*

The *Eleanor Lancaster* finally set sail again and arrived in Sydney on the 26th of April 1850, but it was hardly the end of the San Francisco adventure for the captain and Emily. They departed, once again, on the 29th of August for San Francisco via Honolulu. William Jackson Barry writes in great detail in his book, *"Past and Present, and Men of the Times"* of this passage to San Francisco. An old acquaintance of the captain (possibly a relative Lodge's first wife, also a Barry), he had been *"favored"* thus receiving a berth on board the ship. The *Eleanor Lancaster* was reportedly terribly overcrowded and *"men had been taken aboard like sheep."* It seems that as there was a *"tolerable admixture of doubtful characters"* on board, many uncomfortable situations ensued. There were fights over provisions, robberies and numerous other antics. Barry confided often with the captain and warned him of mutinous characters. Upon landing at Honolulu, many of the rowdier individuals found themselves in trouble and locked up by the authorities, and the ship sailed on to San Francisco without them. Perhaps it was a good thing for Emily to finally reach land; to disembark the rowdies and to get a whiff of some fresh air—as the ship had also carried cattle and horses and may have been a little ripe after so many months' journey.

According to *Shipping Intelligence,* the *Eleanor Lancaster* arrived at Sydney on April 2, 1851. The Lodges were not long on land for they were off again—this time for China. Only *Mrs. Lodge and family and a servant* were listed as passengers. This trip proved to generate much controversy in Newcastle. The *Eleanor Lancaster* arrived back in

Newcastle with Mrs. Lodge and family and sixty-seven Chinese laborers. A public meeting was summoned in Newcastle concerning these Chinese laborers. There was a great need for labor at the time. Some felt the Chinese were brought to Australia as slaves, and found the whole idea abhorrent. Others were concerned that they would bring vile and pagan behaviors to Australia. Still others felt that if they could do the work then they would be welcome. Captain Lodge and the *Eleanor Lancaster* were mentioned often throughout the meeting and one gentleman, Mr. Simon Kemp, admitted that he would like to invite Captain Lodge to a public dinner for bringing his vessel of Chinese laborers to this port. However, most of those present believed that the introduction of Chinese laborers would *"impede the social, moral and political advancement of the colony and compromise the character of the free British subjects, abhorring slavery in any form."*

The story of the Chinese laborers contains one mystery, however, and it rests in the lines of the passenger record…*Mrs. Lodge and family*… According to all family records, the union of Captain Lodge and Emily produced no issue. It seems almost hard to believe that even as Emily had accompanied her husband on almost every voyage throughout their marriage, no children were born unto them. Could *"and family"* reveal the possibility that there had been children who never lived to adulthood but had accompanied them to China? Childbirth and infancy were two dangerous situations on board a 19th century ship. Usually babies were delivered hastily by the captain, or their father-- and more often than not women died in childbirth. Infants had little or no chance of building the natural immunities to disease as they were unhealthily sheltered on a ship for months at a time. Their first encounters on land usually proved fatal. Did the captain and Mrs. Lodge have children who had died at sea? It is very possible, but to this day, it is a fact unknown.

After returning from China new owners took over the *Eleanor Lancaster* and Captain Lodge gave her up and went to England to become a salvager with the Marine Insurance Company.

Unfortunately, the *Eleanor Lancaster* was soon wrecked in a gale on Oyster Bank, Newcastle, New South Wales, on November 7, 1856, and forever memorialized in a poem, *"Perilous Gate."* Captain Lodge's new position brought the couple to a new sort of life at London's Broad Street area. The 1861 census of England reveals they were living with Lodge's parents and family in Middlesex. According to Sir Oliver Lodge, his uncle was *"one who organized the salvage of sunken vessels and the recovery of any treasure which they might contain."* Captain Lodge was skillful at these operations and was much entrusted with the priceless treasures that were inevitably sought after and found. Various shipwrecks he was known to work on included: *the Schiller, the Royal Charter, Hamilla Mitchell and the Alphonso XII*. However, it was the treasures of the *S. S. Golden Gate* that brought Emily to Niagara Falls and her final resting place at Oakwood.

The *S.S. Golden Gate*, part of the Pacific Mail Steamship fleet, ran aground about 300 yards from shore in Manzanillo, Mexico. A fire had broken out on Sunday, July 27, 1862, between the engines and the aft gallery, while the crew and passengers were sitting down to dinner. It had left San Francisco with 338 passengers and crew plus 1.4 million dollars in gold, bound for Panama. It was also rumored to have carried an additional million dollars' worth of gold in the purser's storage. A total loss by fire, with 213 dead…legend soon grew around the wreck. For many months bodies, possessions and gold washed upon the shores. Several salvage companies immediately came to the area to retrieve any remains and valuables. Two men, Thomas Smiley and another, a captain known only as Irelan, mounted their own personal salvage expeditions and retrieved an estimated $300,000. Smiley was soon arrested and prosecuted in San Francisco. The Salvage Association of Lloyd's of London immediately sent Captain Lodge as representative and Special Agent. It was believed that Smiley had unlawfully pirated the gold and the British underwriters were not prepared to let so much money get away. Letters and journal pages exist today and have been transcribed and made public by descendants of Captain Lodge, Kim and Robin Patterson. One letter expresses the well wishes of I. A. W. Harper, as the Lodges prepared to leave England for work on the *S.S. Golden Gate*. *"A Pleasant Voyage! And Success!"* A passenger record reveals that Captain Lodge and Emily H. sailed from Liverpool, on board the *Canada*, to Mexico via Boston. They arrived on December 14, 1863. It is unknown if they did make it to Mexico as the United States was in the heat of the Civil War and it may have been difficult passage. According to the letters, Captain and Mrs. Lodge proceeded on to San Francisco where Lodge became deeply embroiled in court instead of working on the wreck of the *S. S. Golden Gate*. The family documents from 1863-1865 are rich in detail, however, without mention of Emily. The charges were dropped against Smiley in August of 1864 in return for payment of $40,000 to Lloyd's. The notes seem to end here after August 26th 1864, and then pick up again, after several months absence, on March 10, 1865. Francis and Emily must have taken a holiday, for on October 1st, *Mr. F.W. Lodge and wife* had signed the guest register at the Cataract Hotel in Niagara Falls, New York, where Emily would die but nine days afterwards, so ending the story of Emily Helena. She was thirty six years old.

Although exact details are not available, careful reconstruction of those last nine days leading up to her unfortunate death is possible as various journals and reminiscences exist. The beginning of October of 1864 found the weather treacherous. Snow blanketed the ground. However, weather did not often stop the traveler to Niagara. It is easy to imagine that they had visited the most common attractions available to tourists in the fall of 1864. There were myriads of curiosities for sale every which way they turned and beadwork of the local squaws and other souvenirs flooded the pathway to the great cataract. Did she stop and buy some? What caught her eye? There was the walk across the suspension bridge to Goat Island, a brave glance down into the rapids beneath them, the indescribable falls, *'the little bits of red coloring that made everything look twice as beautiful,"* a *"horrible ferry"* to the Canadian side and *"a moon twice as bright"* as a normal moon. There were men and women holding hands, clinging close, whispering forever vows to one another. There was a last glance, a last kiss, a last meal, a last song.

The Cataract House, where they spent their quiet time, kept a strangely mixed staff of freed black servers in white jackets and aprons and Irish housemaids who overtly loathed the North and sympathized with the rebels' cause. Table d'hote dining was conveniently available at the Cataract at various times through the day. A small menu of interesting items was advertised. Although most of the menu detailed the various spirits offered, dinners consisted of meals such as oxtail soup, kidney au fine herbs, calves feet, a la St. Menue, various pastries and cabinet pudding. What were her choices for her last meal? Did they share a glass of wine? Each waiter was provided with wine cards and pencil. The captain and his wife needed only to fill it in and soon enough tables would rumble softly, crystal would hum a faint swan song, and glasses would be brought to lips. Perhaps Emily had also spent a moment or two with the other guests in the ladies parlor. There were chairs, iced water and tumblers and a very *bad piano*. It is likely that she had run her fingers across the keys, one last time, while the captain had a smoke and liquored up in the bar.

It is possible that the Cave of the Winds—that perilous trip underneath the American Falls—was the culprit that hastened the demise of Emily Helena. Was it the beginning of the end? The Cave of the Winds was the spectacle most Victorian tourists did not want to miss. Did they laugh at the sight of the other in the *"queerest, oddest looking scantiest set of garments?"* Were they led Indian file down some steps and directly into the spray of the cataract? With their hands, their fingernails, did they cling to the slimy rock, fearing the end of their lives? Did they feel the thunder, as the sheets of water hissed and roared? Did it drive the breath from their bodies? Maybe it was here, in the Cave of the Winds, that Henu first caught sight of her. The Plessos women most certainly had a long history of catching the eye of both men and gods. Did he know she was coming?

I imagine her death was miserable and agonizing. Surely, the hotel doctor would have attended to her and prescribed the strongest of bitters. But her body was tired. Did Henu rustle her curtains, await her moment of weakness? *"Awake or asleep there is no escape,"* writes one traveler. Emily shut her eyes one last time to the echoes of the thundering anthem.

There is a chance our strange introduction to Emily was not an accident at all. Although her body is long gone another more powerful part of her survives. Thanks to Mrs. Crummer, of Cammeray, New South Wales, we now have a photograph of this remarkable woman from the other side of the world. The wife of Emily's last living relative graciously sent a copy of a daguerreotype to my home in Niagara Falls. Mrs. Crummer's late husband, Robert, had been the great grandson of Emily's brother, Robert Sherer. It is a miracle in itself that we can look into Emily's eyes. A puzzle has begun to put itself together.

Sir Oliver Lodge, Emily's nephew, the first man to transmit a message by wireless signal, a pioneer of our modern world of unseen waves of communication: radios, televisions, the internet—through his research into the paranormal, understood the world of the invisible. Absolutely convinced of the survival of man and a skillful communicator with other realms of reality, he wrote that he would *"rejoice in the opportunity of service of use by Higher Powers."* It was said that mediums often broke through in the form of one of his deceased aunts or uncles during the sessions of the British Society of Psychical Research (SPR). I can only wonder if Emily had made herself known during these sessions. It is possible, that if such things really do exist, Sir Oliver Lodge may have had a hand in the events which have transpired at Oakwood Cemetery. However, it is also possible that everything was just a series of coincidences…But to those of us involved, the story of Emily is one of myth and magic, of rebirth and resurrection; a tale written by Niagara, herself.

"Thou art not to be got rid of as easily as the stars…" Margaret Fuller

Chapter Three
Niagara's Lost Lovers;
Lottie Philpott and Ethelbert Parsons

The newspapers called it, *The Niagara Falls Horror*—for what occurred on August 9, 1875, was one of Niagara's most melancholy tragedies.

It began just as any other summer's day. A group of young revelers visited the Cave of the Winds at about half past five o'clock. It was said that they chose that hour for at *"no hour of the day can the rainbow be seen to such perfection."* The party passed through the cave and over the bridges in front of the American fall. Although they had been warned by the guides of possible calamity resulting from entering the water, they clamored over the rocks until reaching a natural basin area. This natural basin was considered by locals to be a *"safe"* bathing place— although in reality the currents were quite treacherous.

Miss Philpott entered the water first, with Mr. Parsons following behind. They held hands and amused themselves in the water...all the while beholding the danger and the romance of the scene that had unveiled itself before them. But the grandeur of the moment was short-lived for the slippery rocks were not easy to set foot upon with such violent currents wreaking havoc on the waters. At once, Lottie lost her footing and slipped. Her mishap took Mr. Parsons down as well. They were both caught and whirled downward with great rapidity. No matter how hard they tried it was impossible to retain a foothold as the stones were slippery and slimy. At one point Mr. Parsons was thrown into an eddy near the shore and he could have saved himself—but instead he rushed back into the foaming rapids— hoping to rescue Miss Philpott. Finally, he did miraculously catch her but *"the mighty Niagara grasped them and hurried them down the spray and foam towards Prospect Park."*

At last they were separated and Miss Philpott went down holding up her hands—*"a shower of spray intervened and when it lifted nothing remained but clouds of foam and water."* Parsons suffered a similar fate. *"From the shore he was seen struggling in an aimless way to keep his head above the water. A thick cloud of spray intervened for a moment between the drowning man and the friends who were powerless to lend him aid and when it disappeared Parsons was gone, and the cruel river swept on as though this tragedy had not been."*

Their bodies were found a few days following the ghastly event surfacing near the Canadian shoreline. Although bloated and discolored, they were identified by friends and family. Miss Philpott's body was found first. It was in such a terrible state that it was impossible to bring home for a proper viewing. Instead, the remains were taken to the vault in Oakwood Cemetery as soon as possible. Funeral services were held at the Presbyterian Church and the choir from St. Peter's Episcopal, of which Miss Philpott was also connected, chanted the burial service at her grave at Oakwood. Mr. Parsons' badly decomposed body was soon after dragged to shore. His remains were also placed in the vault at Oakwood. Funeral services were held at his mother's home in LaSalle and his body was taken to Buffalo for interment.

The Niagara Falls Gazette so beautifully finalized the tragedy of the death of Lottie Philpott and Ethelbert Parsons in their issue published on August 18, 1875. No other words can more perfectly sum up the tale of Niagara's most tragic lovers....

"Such a casualty would be sad in any case; it is rendered doubly so when the victims are both residents of the town—young people who have grown up to womanhood and manhood among our citizens. Mr. Parsons was the son of the late Horatio A. Parsons, Esq., and was a young gentleman of fine promise and more than an average ability. Miss Lottie C. Philpott, was the only daughter of a respectable citizen of Niagara Falls. She was twenty-five years of age and was widely known for the beauty of her person and character. The fact that she was soon to be led to the altar by the man who went to his death with her, invests her untimely fate with an almost weirdly romantic interest..."

Chapter Four

The Silver Drinking-cup of Death;

Mathilde Rolland

Monsieur and Madame Rolland were supposed to return to New York early that morning in June of 1879. Instead, they decided to have one last look at Niagara Falls…which was unfortunate for Madame Rolland.

The Rolland's, of 24 Rue Mognau, Paris, France, had been on a world tour. In fact, since their marriage in Paris two years prior to the tragedy, their lives were said to have been a *"continual honeymoon."* Monsieur Rolland, a 44 year old wealthy gunsmith from Belgium, and his wife, Mathilde, a 25 year old exceptionally beautiful young woman expecting their first child, had visited China, Japan, San Francisco, and Chicago before finally coming to Niagara Falls. They roomed at the Falls Hotel and as they could speak but little English took most of their meals at a French restaurant kept by a fellow countryman, J.B. Romain. They visited all of the usual places of interest and were to start back for New York. At the last moment, however, Madame Rolland changed plans. She had been so taken in by the majesty of one particular spot on Goat Island that she would not leave without a farewell visit. They left their hotel around nine in the morning and walked over the bridge, stopping at Luna Island. They also revisited the Cave of the Winds and the point formerly occupied by the Terrapin tower. Finally they moved on to the Three Sister Islands. They passed on from the first Sister and to the second Sister. By the steps near the third Sister, in the area between the third Sister and the island that is impossible to access (known as Little Brother), Madame Rolland became obsessed with the spectacle of a little boy that she seemed to see off in the distance. She watched as he ran about the islands and then as he dipped a cup into the river, which he drank from. Madame Rolland followed after him and was suddenly struck with a strange desire to take a drink from Niagara, too. When she found a good spot to dip into she asked her husband for his silver drinking-cup which he carried in his breast pocket. After giving it to her he stepped back, for he found a view that he was compelled to contemplate. A few moments passed and then the solitude was broken with a resounding shriek. Madame Rolland had fallen into the water. He rushed to the edge only to see her washed away upon the crest of the descending river. At one point he saw her appear a few rods below. She arose three times throwing her hands up and screaming for help before she disappeared.

"Her white face was for an instant turned heavenward, and the next instant her body was caught in the resistless fury of the undertow and she was swept away forever…"

Monsieur Rolland, having no idea what to do, rushed madly back to Romain's restaurant screaming: *My God! My God! My wife, my darling Mathilde!*

He explained what had transpired and soon after watches were set to recover the body.

A few days later Madame Rolland's remains were discovered by a fisherman on the Canadian shore. Coroner McGarry of Drummondville was notified. The body was totally nude, with the exception of the shoes and stockings, a black lace neck-tie and a glove on the left hand. Upon removal of the glove, Madame Rolland's wedding ring was found encircling the third finger. No bones were broken, however, the right shoulder appeared to be dislocated. It was found remarkable that her remains were still in such an excellent state of preservation. Monsieur Romain and his wife were able to positively identify the body as Monsieur Rolland was on his way back to Paris.

Madame Rolland's final chapter was not so idyllic. Like many others, she was a traveler with a one-way ticket to Niagara Falls. Her body, left for over 12 hours in the summer heat, partly out of the water, with the head and shoulders mercilessly tossed by the boisterous waves, was in quite a dismal state upon removal. When the body was finally towed down to the ferry landing and placed within the coffin it presented a most horrific sight. Those few hours had wreaked havoc on poor Madame Rolland. She was prepared for burial by undertaker E.M. Clark and her remains taken to St. Mary's Church where Father Lanigan conducted funeral services. She was finally buried in the new Catholic Cemetery that had been a part of Oakwood.

Monsieur Romain telegraphed the New York agent of the French line of steamers hoping to find Monsieur Rolland and to explain to him what had occurred since his departure. He was able to make contact eventually but all that Mathilde's husband was able to say was that he was very appreciative of Romain's assistance however he could not wait to sail from the country where this horrible calamity occurred.

    **It must be mentioned that there were those in the city of Niagara Falls who believed it may just have been possible that Monsieur Rolland's story was not completely true. For the water in those parts plays a perfect alibi for situations involving foul play.

Chapter Five

The Cementation of the Dead; Theodore Graves Hulett

He spent his boyhood by the light of tallow candles, pouring over whatever books he could get his hands on. He was mechanical by nature. Never satisfied. Always seeking more knowledge and that light in the darkness. Born into meager circumstances on June 13, 1811, in Williamsburgh, Massachusetts, Theodore Graves Hulett left home at twelve years old to apprentice with a carriage manufacturer in Pittsfield. He taught himself law on the side and eventually made his way to Niagara Falls by 1834. An important man, he was superintendent of the first Suspension Bridge and constructed the famous iron basket which, at one time, was the only means of transportation between the United States and Canada at this point until the bridge was created. It was suspended on a cable that ran along the American and Canadian shores. He was so confident in its durability that he sent his own daughter across on its maiden voyage—never imagining for a moment the possibility that it could tumble down into the gorge taking little Elvira to a most violent death. In 1849, Hulett was elected Justice of the Peace of the town of Niagara. He was extremely active in most public matters in Niagara Falls and was one of our most prominent and respected residents. During the Civil War he took care of the soldiers and their families. But there was one more thing about Judge Hulett. It was probably one of the most unusual contributions anyone ever made to Niagara Falls. He originated the idea of and practiced (in Oakwood Cemetery) the cementation of the dead.

No one is certain exactly how many graves and individuals were cemented as records are sparse during this time period. According to news articles of the time, *"cementation of the dead"* was pretty common practice after 1886—but only in Oakwood Cemetery. It was the only cemetery in the world to dispose of the dead in this manner. According to a Niagara Gazette article on August 31, 1886, *"this mode of burial has become the rule in Oakwood Cemetery."* It cost the families an additional fee of $15 *"to cement a casket in a stone casing of eight inches in thickness and without a royalty as it was under a scientist's patent."* Apparently, *"on account of the moisture in the ground..."* Oakwood Cemetery was the perfect location for the cementation of the dead.

It was on June 4, 1874, that Judge Hulett first obtained some frogs, prepared a cement mixture and cemented the frogs into stone blocks. He did the same with a pear. Five years later he sawed them open and found the most amazing thing had occurred. The watery portions of the once living material had been absorbed by the stone, leaving the tissues intact and a perfect cast of the original. Even much of the original colors remained. He kept these specimens on exhibition in his office for many years. It was in 1874 that he wrote out his last will and testament in which he gave specific orders for the cementation of his own body.

In 1886, before the Sanitary Board in Buffalo, Judge Hulett declared that *"he had decided to cement all his family."* His two daughters feeling the cementation of their bodies would be *"pretty close quarters"* requested that only their coffins be encased in cement to the thickness of a foot. Each box weighed two tons. Others would have three inches of cement placed in their coffin and allowed to harden. At this point the embalmed nude body would be laid upon the foundation and the coffin filled with cement until the body was three inches below the surface. The graves dug for the cementation process would be much deeper in order to receive the casket. More cement would be poured over the lowered casket and fine sulphur and powdered charcoal with alcohol would then be placed between the outer case and the casket and then set on fire. The lid would then be screwed on. This process would ensure that all liquids in the body be absorbed and the gases from the dead body neutralized. It was believed that the cementation of the dead would secure the body from the attacks of grave robbers. Or perhaps from something more sinister than grave robbers...

The first cementation of a body in Oakwood Cemetery occurred in January of 1887. David Hulett Thomas, a relative of Judge Hulett, after having been mysteriously killed in the railroad yards, was the first to be buried by the unique process. Representatives from the

IOOF (Independent Order of Odd Fellows) and the fire companies of Niagara Falls, New York, and Niagara Falls, Ontario, of which the deceased was a member, attended in great numbers--so did representatives of the Health Department, various scientific organizations from around the state and the general public. Following the burial of David Thomas, many of Niagara's dead were buried in the same fashion in Oakwood Cemetery.

The cementation of the dead in Oakwood Cemetery was Judge Hulett's one last obsession in his twilight years. He was the founder and president of the American Cementation Society, which was established in Buffalo, and the editor of *"the Cemetarian,"* a monthly newsletter concerning topics relating to the cementation of the dead. Upon his death, on April 13, 1907, Hulett left explicit instructions for the disposal of his own body. He greatly preferred *"Portland Cement"* over all others *"as long as it can be obtained at a reasonable price."* A Unitarian, he requested that a Universalist minister be present for the service but if that was not available *"any clergyman or layman"* may do as long as he leads in a favorite hymn by Cowper. Perhaps the oddest part of his Hulett's request was the simplest. He asked that the only *"representative"* of his body at the funeral be his *"easy chair, empty,"* his *"cane and boots lying in the chair"* and his *"grand and great grandchildren standing (or sitting) around the chair and other friends standing or sitting around in an outer circle..."*

It is possible that Hulett's strange fascination with making certain the dead would not rise again lies somewhere within the annals of the history of Niagara Falls--for there was a singular event that occurred in July of 1866 in the yards of the Central Railroad, near the Suspension Bridge that could explain his obsession. The event caused much excitement and certainly piqued the wild imagination of Niagara's residents. Newspapers across the nation became interested in the reports that 60-70 sheep had been found killed, in most unusual circumstances over a few days' time near Niagara Falls. Even as these animals commonly roamed freely throughout the village an occurrence such as this was most startling for the fact that *"the sheep were merely bitten in the neck and the blood sucked from the carcass."* No other damage had been done to their bodies. A posse was formed and men with torches were sent out to search for the guilty varmints.

Outwardly, it was supposed that a wolf had been the culprit, although it had been believed that the last remnants of wolves had been eradicated years before. The culprit was never discovered although it seems possible that the villagers felt a supernatural presence had made itself known. The general public, at the time, was well aware of vampires and their proclivities. Even as Bram Stoker's, *Dracula*, had yet to be written, the short story, *"The Vampyre"*, conceived by John Polidori, Lord Byron's physician, in 1819, was popular literature throughout the United States.

People will always be fearful of the unknown—and is it possible that this was the case in Niagara Falls? Hulett spent the rest of his life ensuring that the dead of Niagara Falls would rest in peace. Perhaps he knew what had happened to those sheep…perhaps he saw himself as a sort of pioneer *"vampire hunter."* Whatever the answer, we will never know for certain; he has surely taken it to his cemented grave at Oakwood Cemetery.

Chapter Six

Little Miss Rough-on-Rats;

Minnie Scott

It was strange how we first met. It was Sunday and gray and bitter cold in Oakwood Cemetery. Pete was unable to meet us but had emailed her location. My gloves were on and off as I checked and rechecked my phone for the exact spot and not unlike afternoon callers my husband and I wandered around looking for her. Then there she was.

Her grave wasn't very startling at all. In fact I realized that I had seen it many times before and really had never thought much of it. Very common, very nonchalant, she has been entombed here for over a century—never once letting out her dirty little secret. How could I have known?

The whole thing was hard to believe but it is these little intersections in time and space that make my work so enjoyable. Actually, the truth is that I had found Minnie's story by accident. I was looking for someone else and then there she was with that terrible headline in the Niagara Falls Gazette: *"Ill Health Causes Mrs. Scott to End Her Life by Taking Poison—Swallowed Half a Box of Rough on Rats Yesterday Morning and Kept Her Act a Secret."* It was spring time in Niagara Falls but it is not always a happy time for those with the heavy burden. It was May 22, 1907, and for Minnie Scott it was *"the end."* I can't even remember what I was actually looking for now. Minnie's story seemed far more interesting but unfortunately I had other things to do so I mentioned her to a friend and tucked her little headline away until later.

Little did I know that something amazing and unexplainable was in motion for just about two days after discovering little Miss *Rough on Rats* I opened my email and there she was again! Lori Y. (Minnie's great great granddaughter) randomly sent me a message requesting that I find her grandmother's grave and take a photograph of it. When I realized that the grave in question belonged to the same woman I had just found accidentally only a few days before I was compelled to tell the great great granddaughter what had happened. I was curious why she had suddenly felt the need to request her photograph. She said she works in a middle school in Maine and had just finished reading a book called, *The Black Duck*, which deals with a rum-running incident and it made her think of her Niagara Falls ancestors.

She went on to tell of the incredible tragedies that befell her family, Minnie's family, from as far back as her father had remembered. In fact, Oakwood's own Pete Ames had researched this most unusual family a few years before and had sent his work on to Lori. He had forgotten about that until now. So he dug into his old case files and together we brought little Miss *Rough on Rats* back to life.

Of course my first question was: Why? Why not suicide in Niagara Falls? And what the heck is *Rough on Rats*? I found that *Rough on Rats* was a popular rat poison composed mostly of arsenic. It was sprinkled on bread and scooped into saucers. Rats would be enticed and then succumb shortly after gobbling it up. It also worked on mice and mosquitoes and all sorts of other vermin. But when consumed by humans it produces the most vile symptoms and usually (if enough is ingested) results in certain death. Strangely, during Victorian times it was the drug of choice for those considering suicide. It was cheap (only fifteen cents a box) and readily available. A quick glance through the newspapers of the time period reveals an incredible amount of suicides and *"accidents"* with *Rough on Rats*. There were the two little children who thought a slice of bread sprinkled with *Rough on Rats* was a piece of cake. The physician was unable to save them. There was also a miserable story from Lockport of a cook who mistakenly sprinkled *Rough on Rats* into his soup pot and served the poison up to the unknowing canal workers. Perhaps the story that gripped me the most was the one about a young mother who, in the throes of absolute poverty, spent her last fifteen cents on a box of *Rough on Rats*, fed them to her babies (mixed in their cereal) and consumed the rest herself. She claimed she had no other choice as they were all starving to death. She survived but her infants did not and she was charged with murder. Other stories involved shunned lovers and men and women with murderous intent; all of them sprinkling the nefarious powder into drinks and stews. *Rough on Rats* came to symbolize the final act of desperation. And it was the final screen call for Niagara's Minnie Scott.

Minnie (Preuster) Scott was born in July of 1863 to German immigrants and lived (as far as we can tell) her entire life within a few miles of the rush of the falls. She was one of six children and her father was a barber. On June 27, 1881, she married a railroad man with an impressive name, Walter B. Scott. By May of 1882, Minnie gave birth to little Charles W. Scott. But things were less than idyllic for the following notice appeared in the Niagara Falls Gazette in 1883:

This is to give notice that my wife has left my bed and board without cause and I shall pay no bills of her contracting after this date…

This sort of notice was commonplace in 19th century newspapers but I was shocked to see it nonetheless. It leaves much room for the imagination. Were there marital problems? Or was this the beginning of her *illness?* Things must have remedied themselves, though, for by 1884, Minnie and Walter were the proud parents of a little girl, Hattie A. In 1887, another child was born, Albert, and somewhere in between there was a child who died in infancy. Sometimes I think it was that little child's death that may have brought on years of melancholy. For how does one ever get over that? Today we have therapists and counselors and anti-depressants. In Minnie's world there was nothing to comfort that kind of pain but death and *Rough on Rats*. Apparently, according to the account of her death, she had been *ill* for quite some time. In fact, just the year before she had unsuccessfully attempted suicide by *"slashing the arteries of her wrists."* She recovered and was sent to Dr. Crego's Sanitarium (the New York State Asylum for the Insane at Buffalo) and spent much of the year (May through September) recovering under his care. Incidentally, Dr. Floyd Crego was most well known as the oddball criminal psychologist who was called upon to examine Leon Czolgosz following his assassination of President McKinley at the Pan American Exposition in 1901. Dr. Crego often used hypnosis and the measurements of patient's heads to diagnose disease. Unfortunately, Minnie was not one of his success stories.

Minnie died at her home at Cleveland Avenue at five minutes to four. She had ingested the poison the morning before and told no one of her situation. Upon becoming violently ill, Dr. Leo-Wolf was summoned but he could not diagnose her illness. Finally, she made her confession at bedside and told those around that she had taken the *Rough on Rats* with suicidal intent.

Minnie was only 44 at the time of her death and her tombstone is still as fresh and clear as if it were planted yesterday. I will always pass her grave and wish her some sort of happiness, our own little *Miss Rough on Rats*. May you rest in peace, Minnie.

Chapter Seven

Will the "real" Maud

Willard please stand up?

It's true that Niagara is a playful little schemer. Whenever she is bored she calls for those careless souls; the ones that think they can beat her at her own game. They tempt her, push her and prod her. She lets them think they are invincible—for a moment. But they most likely will find themselves entrenched within a watery grave at Oakwood Cemetery.

Such is the sad tale of Miss Maud Willard, a twenty-seven year old dance hall actress *supposedly* from Canton, Ohio.

Maud Willard—or whatever her name actually was—first came into the limelight in August of 1901. She carried the headlines across the country and shocked everyone who read them.

"DOUBLE TURN IN THE WHIRLPOOL'S RAIDS TO BE DONE BY A GIRL AND CARLISLE GRAHAM, THE HERO OF NIAGARA!"

She was to go through the Niagara rapids in Carlisle Graham's barrel—starting, of course, from Graham's favorite point. Graham would give the signal to set the craft afloat and when he was sure she was in full grasp of the current, he was to hurry to the whirlpool on an electric car specially engaged. He would watch the barrel and should it venture out to the outlet of the great river pocket, he would leap into the river and swim to Lewiston, four miles below, with it. However, should she be rescued in the pool, he proclaimed he would make the trip to Lewiston alone.

It was all so well planned. How could anything go wrong? Carlisle Graham was the fearless father of the barrel stunters. A cooper by trade, he originated the idea of crafting a sturdy barrel-- made of oak wood--capable of surviving the tumultuous Niagara Rapids—that could also comfortably fit a man, or a woman. He is recorded to have gone through the rapids five times.   Graham's first trip, on July 11, 1886, was the first barrel stunt at Niagara Falls.   His most dangerous attempt was in July of 1901 when he was trapped in an eddy.   It is believed that it was during this July spectacle that Miss Maud first met up with Graham.   His barrel trip *"aroused the ambition of Miss Maud Willard"* to such an extent that she suddenly was taken in with the notion to make a similar trip.   It was to take place on September 7, 1901.   She would take her little dog…and it was all to be captured on film.

However, things did not go as planned.   First of all the nation was in a state of melancholy as the president clung to dear life after being shot at the Pan-American Exposition in Buffalo.   But the pandemonium did not set Graham and Maud back from going ahead with their stunt.   Maud and her little fox terrier were first cast adrift around 3:58.   By 4:04 the barrel had entered the whirlpool. Normally the customary flow of the water made it so that barrels and boats could be captured and withdrawn from this area after about an hour.   Unfortunately for Miss Willard it wasn't until 9:00 pm when her barrel was finally pulled in.   Upon opening the lid, the dog jumped out but Miss Maud was lifeless.   Captain Johnson, a famous surf swimmer, worked over her for two hours without success and after that a doctor pronounced her dead.   Local lore persists that the dog had stuck his nose in the only breathing hole thereby contributing to her death.

An account of the scene of Maud's death from the Cataract Journal illustrates an horrific nightmare:

"The body was bruised in many places, the lips were blue and the facial expression denoted great suffering….The removal of her body was like a scene from Dante's, Inferno. Proceeding under torchlight, a team of laborers, riotously intoxicated, dragged Willard's body up the steep bank, pulling it by the ankles, yanking it by the hair, cursing and blaspheming as they groped their way, stumbling, up the rocky, wooded slope. When they

reached the top, another drunken reveler was found asleep in the wooden coffin reserve for Willard's corpse..."

It was the last hurrah for the dance hall actress. Her body was transported to Oakwood Cemetery. She was survived by her mother, a son and two sisters—all of whom resided in Niagara Falls at the time of her demise.

But the story of Maud Willard did not end with her death that fateful day in September of 1901. In fact it had only just begun. While researching her antics over one hundred years later a few news articles and a document changed everything we had ever known about the young woman who did not survive her barrel trick in the Niagara River. Maud Willard, as she had been known, did not actually exist. When the story of her planned trip circulated through the newswires efforts were made to investigate her background. She did not appear in Canton city directories, nor did anyone in Canton seem to know of her existence...until a savvy reporter from the local newspaper located a Mrs. Willard White, nee Maud M. Hann, who had just returned from a visit to Cleveland, Detroit and Buffalo. She claimed that her friends had known her as *"Maud Willard"*—a name she had created after combining her first name with her husband's first name. She declined to discuss details of her stunt at Niagara Falls, but stated that she was truly the woman who would be doing the job.

Strangely...following the incident of her supposed death in the Niagara rapids, that same reporter decided to venture back to Mrs. Willard White's household and as unbelievable as it must have been for him—he found her alive and at home! The husband would only speak for the wife and he admonished the fact that he *"could not tell how it came about that the woman drowned at Niagara was supposed to be Maud Willard of Canton..."*

No follow-up story has come to our attention however upon obtaining the official death record for *Maud Willard*...yet another mystery was born. The woman who died in Carlisle Graham's barrel, who perished by "*suffocation*," was not "*Maud Willard*" but "*Maud Wilson*." Other details on the official record state that she was indeed an actress, born in Springfield, Ohio, to George Literman and Allie Whitman. Incidentally, Maud's mother, "*Allie Whitman*," was said to have died from "*a broken heart*" just about one month following her daughter's tragic end. A forty-eight year old widow, her death record does impart that she died of "*heart failure*." She was buried up the road from her daughter in Oakwood Cemetery.

Perhaps one day the story of "*Maud Willard*" will have a *happily ever after*...but for now it is apparently without end.

Chapter Eight

She was Demented;

Caroline Rank

It is a little known fact that librarians are often bearers of great secrets. People come to us with their burdens, their sadness—always seeking solace and answers to the most difficult questions. It was said that Francis Abbott, the *Hermit of Niagara,* who perished in the river in 1831, confided only in the librarian, Samuel DeVeaux. It was no different during the bleak and final weeks of 1912. For it was just the day before Thanksgiving that Mrs. Caroline Rank, widow and former resident of Washington, D.C., first approached Miss Maud Cathcart, Niagara Falls librarian.

Mrs. Rank, hysterical and demented—had visited Niagara Falls in years past on numerous occasions accompanied by her husband. Following his death, it was said that she had been treated several times for nervous disorders in sanitariums. She was paranoid, frantic, despondent. Upon being released she had only one desire—and that was to return to Niagara Falls.

Never certain of her safety, she bounced from boarding house to boarding house. She stayed with Miss Cathcart for some time at her home at First Street—but left abruptly after complaining that *"someone had designs on her life."* She was also noted to have lodged with Miss Catherine McCabe of Third Street.

Most of Mrs. Rank's final days were spent within the library, conversing with the librarians. *Just another crazy!*—the librarians probably laughed amongst themselves. But on Saturday morning, December 10, 1912, the situation took a dark turn. Mrs. Rank was even more agitated than usual. She related to Miss Cathcart how she had found out exactly how she was to be killed…*it was by poison…they would get her by poison…* Miss Cathcart tried to calm her but left for the day when her shift was up. Not so lucky was poor Mrs. Martha Benham! The other librarian on duty was forced to put up with Mrs. Rank's antics until closing. She tried to go about her daily routine while at the same time dealing with Mrs. Rank.

According to accounts afterwards, Mrs. Benham revealed that it was just about the time she found herself engaged with another patron that Mrs. Rank had disappeared. All seemed eerily calm as Mrs. Benham locked up for the weekend. But unfortunately, all was not calm, for Mrs. Caroline Rank had ventured down into the privacy of the auditorium when no one was watching. She had gone behind the piano that stood upon the stage and fired her revolver into her mouth. Only her head projected from beyond the piano. Her body was partly covered by a chair on which she had left a piece of fancy work. Inside a glove on her hand was found a note with this inscription:

I wish to be buried at Niagara Falls. Notify Samuel Ross, Eleventh and C Streets, Washington, D.C., for funeral expenses. Caroline Rank...

Her body was not found until Monday, when a janitor stumbled upon her corpse while cleaning. After a post-mortem examination it was pronounced that Mrs. Rank had died instantly. It was also discovered that she was a woman of considerable wealth. Samuel Ross was the executor of her husband's estate and he was contacted in order to deal with her burial expenses. Upon learning of the incident he awaited further notice. Her body was sent to Dykstra Brothers, Undertakers, and, according to the death record from Niagara Falls, burial was at Watsontown, Pennsylvania. There is a stone at Watsontown Cemetery that commemorates Mrs. Rank's demise:

Carrie Kerr Rank

Died December 12, 1912

Or does it?

In 1982, the Niagara Gazette investigated Mrs. Rank's most unusual finale and reported that the sexton at the cemetery claimed that after searching through burial records found there was *no mention of her ever being buried there.*

So where is she?

Is it possible her restless spirit still haunts the old Carnegie library building in Niagara Falls? Has she returned to Niagara Falls? Numerous ghostly encounters were reported back in the 1980's when the new library was being repaired and it was necessary to house the audio-visual department of the library in the old Carnegie library location. Most activity occurred during the month of December—strangely, the month of Mrs. Rank's suicide.

In the end—Mrs. Rank was quite explicit concerning the details of her final destiny.

I wish to be buried at Niagara Falls.

Perhaps, in a way, as one of *the missed*—one of the forgotten ones—she *was* buried at Niagara Falls. And, perhaps, in a way, our knowledge of her tragic end——inevitably breathes new life into a dusty old spirit.

Last Lines

All is Change, Eternal Progress, No Death

Francis Abbott

Found chiseled onto a rock on Luna Island.

1831

I will commit suicide in this fall.

An open letter found on the third Sister Island.

Signed: T. Tamal, 12 Concord St., Brooklyn.

March 30, 1907

To the finder: please notify my wife at Cleveland, Ohio, and give her these as identification...

Jules Piccus

June 18, 1832

I will be in the falls not far from where you find this...

Unknown

Over the falls, John Pfeiffer, Pennsylvania...

Written on a four foot fence board in heavy black ink

Outside the Genesee House

June 22, 1896

Man with driving license and other miscellaneous identification papers as George N. Cooper went off the bridge into the river tonight. Please send notice of event...

Telegram sent to Earl F. Colburn, 10 Gibbs Street, Rochester

October 13, 1926

Goodbye, I am gone, F.W.E.

Bottle with a message in it found near the whirlpool

June 20, 1897

...to the finders: please notify police of finding this. My body will be found in the river near this spot.

Kindly see that my watch is forwarded to my wife.

God bless you for your assistance. I am placing in a metal box in my trouser pocket a note of identification similar to that in the leather case in my coat.

J.J. Fitzpatrick

Niagara Falls, Ontario

November 15, 1927

Well I thought that I would end it all by coming here. The water is fast and deep and I cannot swim at all and in this place no one would be so foolish as to try to save anyone after they were once in the water...

Herbert E. McCrorie (alias William D. Mack)

November 30, 1920

Do not look for my body. I am no more...

George Elverson

Written on the top of a page of newspaper

October 11, 1900

I wish to be buried at Niagara Falls...

Caroline Rank

Note found tucked inside her glove after committing suicide inside the Niagara Falls Public Library

December 10, 1912

Bibliography

Anthology and Bibliography of Niagara Falls, Volume 1, by Charles Mason Dow, 1921.

A Description of Lousiana, by Father Louis Hennepin, translated from the edition of 1683, 1880.

The Evolution of an Ethnic Neighborhood that Became United In Diversity: The East Side, Niagara Falls, New York 1880-1930, William H. Feder, Ph.D, 2000.

The Falls of Niagara, or Tourist's Guide to this Wonder of Nature, by Samuel DeVeaux, 1839.

Hen Frigates, Wives of Merchant Captains Under Sail, by Joan Druatt, 1998.

Houdini! The Career of Ehrich Weiss, by Kenneth Silverman, 1996.

Margery the Medium, by James Malcolm Bird, 1925.

Modern American Spiritualism, by Emma Hardinge Britton, 1860.

My Canadian Leaves, An Account of a Visit to Canada in 1864-1865, by Frances E.O. Monck, 1891.

My Inventions, by Nikola Tesla, 1919.

Niagara, A history of the Falls, by Pierre Berton, 1992.

Past and Present and Men of the Times, by William Jackson Barry, 1892.

Past Years, an Autobiography, by Sir Oliver Lodge, 1932.

Shivers Down Your Spine: Panorama and the Origin of Cinematic Reenactment, by Allison Griffiths, 2008.

Soaring Gulls and Bowing Trees; the history of the islands above Niagara Falls, by Paul Gromosiak, 1989.

Studies of the Niagara Frontier, by Frank Severance, 1911.

Voices from Beyond, by Henry Hardwicke, 1930.

Why I Believe the Dead are Alive, by William Dudley Pelley, 1942.

The author, Michelle Ann Kratts,

& the photographer, Michelle Petrazzoulo.

Photo courtesy Tim Baxter.